KidCaps' Presents
Natural Disasters:
Understanding Weather Just for Kids!

KidCaps is An Imprint of BookCaps™
www.KidLito.com

This table of contents makes no sense!

Table of Contents

This page I do not understand

3

5

The Science of Earthquakes

Introduction

The earth is always in motion beneath our feet – bending, squeezing, shifting, pulling and pushing. It's always moving – we just can't feel it. That's because the motion happens deep within the earth. But sometimes it occurs with such substantial force that it causes the rocks that make up the layers of the earth to move. And when this happens, we do feel it. It's what we call an "earthquake." The earth, literally, moves beneath our feet. It quakes.

Here's how it happens: the layer of rock nearest to the surface of the earth, which is called the "lithosphere," is terribly brittle compared to the other layers of rock. It can only bend so far before it breaks. When it breaks, the rock may move. Sometimes the movement is so slight, it is barely noticed. It may just produce a little rumble and some mild shaking in the ground. Other times, it can move a lot, so much that it can shake the ground until buildings and bridges collapse and people are thrown off their feet! This is an earthquake. An earthquake is, put simply, the sudden shaking of the earth caused by movements beneath the earth's surface.

Being in an earthquake can be tremendously scary. The first thing that happens is that there is a deep rumbling sound. Then, the ground begins to tremble and shake. It might only last for a few seconds or it might last for minutes. The movement of the earth may be so minor that it only causes a slight shaking – the movement may cause you to wake you from sleep or make pictures hanging on the wall slip – or it may be so major that it causes buildings, bridges and roads to collapse, and people have to run for their lives!

Each year, more than a million earthquakes occur around the world. While most of them are too small to even notice, others can cause massive destruction, with at least one or two earthquakes every year that are big and that result in major damage.

A powerful earthquake can have a terrible effect on people and their lives. Houses, offices and schools can be destroyed. Hospitals, stores and factories can be wiped out. Roads and bridges may be too damaged to use, so people are trapped where they are. Along with damage to structures, water pipes, power lines and gas pipes can break, and power cables can be knocked down. This can cause fires that then cause further damage to buildings.

Sometimes, so many buildings are damaged in an earthquake that they must be torn down and bulldozed. People are left homeless. They have no utilities. They have no roads or schools or hospitals. It can take a lot of effort and time to rebuild an area after an earthquake. In some cases, it can take several years.

Why do earthquakes happen? What makes the ground suddenly and violently shift under our feet? Let's try to figure that out.

Chapter 1: Where Do Earthquakes Occur?

To understand *why* earthquakes happen, it helps to look first at *where* they happen since they don't happen just anywhere in the world. Some areas in the world, in fact, have never experienced an earthquake. But other areas have experienced a lot of earthquakes. Those areas are known as "earthquake hotspots." They may have several earthquakes every year. Earthquakes happen frequently in these parts of the world for a reason.

Basically, earthquakes occur in zones along the edges of "tectonic plates." They occur in the places where the tectonic plates meet. What are tectonic plates? They are the hulking slabs of rock that make up the surface of the earth, which we noted in the introduction is called the "lithosphere." These large pieces of rocks, or "plates," move over the top of the layer of rock that is under the lithosphere, called the "asthenosphere." The asthenosphere is a subterranean sea of hot and plastic rock. It is able to bend without breaking. There are at least ten large plates and several smaller ones moving over the asthenosphere. These tectonic plates are always in motion.

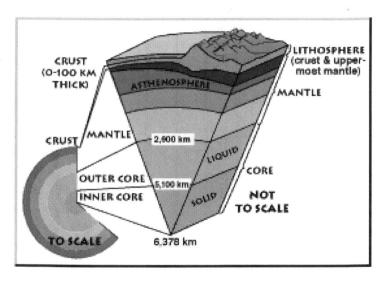

There are two main zones in the world where most earthquakes take place. About 75 percent of the world's earthquakes occur in a zone in the Pacific Ocean, known as the "Ring of Fire." This area also has many active volcanoes. The second zone, where about 25 percent of earthquakes occur, runs from Southeast Asia through the Middle East to the Mediterranean Sea.

Basically, the areas in the world along the edges of the tectonic plates have the most earth-moving activity, whether the result is an earthquake or a volcano. In the highlands of Guatemala, for instance, which is located in Central America, there is a chain of 33 volcanoes located above a coastal plain. This area experiences many earthquakes due to the constant movement of tectonic plates in the region. In recent years, Guatemala has experienced at least one major earthquake every year.

Tectonic Plates

Tectonic plates are in constant motion. They slowly rub against one another, which causes pressure to build beneath the earth's surface. When the pressure builds to a certain point, the plates can jolt against one another, which sends out "shock waves." These shock waves can cause an earthquake. Small earthquakes will only cause the ground to tremble, but large earthquakes can cause the earth's crust to crack and may cause severe damage. Some of the biggest earthquakes happen when one tectonic plate is forced under another. This results in the lower plate grinding into the upper plate, causing the upper plate to shift drastically.

Plates are categorized as "Primary," "Secondary," and "Tertiary."
The primary plates are large and comprise the bulk of the continents
as well as the Pacific Ocean. These include the Eurasian Plate, the
North American Plate, the South American Plate, the Indo-
Australian Plate, the Antarctic Plate, the Pacific Plate and the
African Plate. Secondary plates show up on most plate maps but do
not cover major areas of land. These are the Arabian Plate, the
Caribbean Plate, the Cocos Plate, the Indian Plate, the Juan de Fuca
Plate, the Nazca Plate, the Philippine Sea Plate and the Scotia Plate.
Tertiary plates are small plates that once were part of the larger
plates. There are at least 60 tertiary plates.

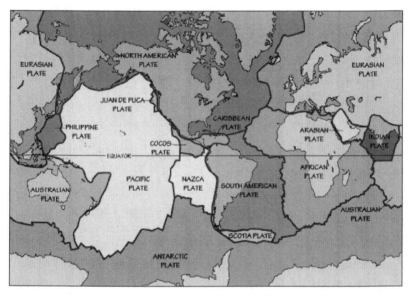

World map of Tectonic Plates.
Image credit: USGS

Chapter 2: What Causes an Earthquake?

The tectonic plates move slowly, at the rate of about 1.4 inches (3.5 cm) a year. Most earthquakes happen along the edges of these plates. The reason for this is that as the plates move, it creates pressure, or "stress," along the edge of the plates. The stress and strain can stretch the rock along the edge of the plates into new shapes and make deep cracks in it. These cracks are known as "faults." We will talk more about faults later. The main thing to understand at this point is that earthquakes happen along these cracks, or faults. Why?

What happens is that the pressure inside the rock grows to such an immensely, due to the stress that the strain along the fault becomes too much, and the rock can suddenly jerk from its new shape and snap back into its original position. When this happens, the energy released shakes the ground. This shaking is known as an earthquake. Earthquakes usually start deep beneath the ground, but they send out strong shock waves in all directions. When these shock waves reach the earth's surface, they cause the ground to shake.

You can imagine how the force of the earth's tectonic plates sliding past each other can cause an earthquake by trying this simple experiment: place the palm of your hand against a smooth, horizontal surface, such as a table top or a floor, and press down. While still pressing down, try to slide your palm along the surface. It's not easy, is it? Your hand jerks and suddenly stops again. Now imagine that your hand and the surface are two rocks pushing against each other. Can you imagine the force? This is how an earthquake starts.

Rock layers and types of faults

The earth's tectonic plates are made up of layers of rock called "strata." If these strata bend and break, they form a crack called a "fault line." Fault lines range in size from just a few inches (centimeters) or to hundreds of miles (kilometers). They may go into rocks deep underground and stretch the span of a continent. The biggest fault lines are found along the edges of plates. There are four types of faults.

Normal fault

A "normal fault" occurs when rocks are pulled apart, and one block slips down. A normal fault runs at a slant, or "diagonally," through the rock. It is the result of rock on either side of a crack being pulled apart. The rock above the fault then slips, or slides, downward.

Reverse fault

A "reverse fault," sometimes referred to as a "thrust fault," occurs when rocks are pushed together. A reverse fault is also diagonal. When two sides of a crack are being pushed together, the rock above the fault is pushed upward, opposite than what happens with a normal fault.

Strike-slip fault

"Strike-slip faults," sometimes referred to as "transform faults," form when blocks of rocks slide past each other. A slip-through fault is not diagonal. It runs straight up and down, or "vertically," through the rock. The rocks on both sides of the fault slip and slide past each other as they move.

Complex fault

A series of adjoining faults that cause rocks to move is many directions forms what is known of as a "complex fault."

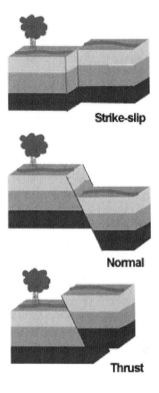

Types of faults.
Image credit: USGS

San Andreas Fault

One of the largest faults in the world is the San Andreas Fault, located in California. It is a transform fault, which means that it was formed when two rocks slid past each other. It is 750 miles (1, 200 kilometers) long. It is located on the boundary of the Pacific and North American plates, about 100 miles north of Los Angeles. These plates move at a rate of about 2 inches (5 centimeters) a year. While Los Angeles in located to the west of the fault, San Francisco – a city that has experienced many major earthquakes – rests almost directly on the fault. This puts San Francisco at risk for serious earthquakes in the future.

Seismic waves

The center of an earthquake is called the "focus," or "hypocenter." This is the place where rocks first jolt together when plates move. The focus may as far as 435 miles (700 kilometers) beneath the surface of the earth. The vibrations that move away from the focus are called "seismic waves," sometimes referred to as "shock waves." These waves travel up to 10 miles (16 kilometers) a second as they move through the ground. As they move away from the focus, they grow weaker, but they can still be quite powerful when they reach the surface. Seismic waves are what cause buildings and bridges to topple and roads to crack. There are different types of seismic waves in two categories: body waves and surface waves.

Body waves

Body waves move through the earth's crust. Primary waves and secondary waves are both body waves. They leave the focus of the earthquake at the same time.

Primary waves

If the body waves travel straight, they are known as primary waves, or "P waves." P waves move at a rate of approximately 2.5 to 4.4 miles per second (4 to 7 km/sec). As they move through rock or liquid, the tiny particles that make up the rock or liquid, known as "molecules," are squeezed together and stretched apart. The motion is similar to the way a coiled spring moves.

Secondary waves

If body waves travel in a snakelike movement, they are known as secondary waves, or "S waves." S waves move slower than P waves. They travel at a rate of approximately 1.2 to 3.1 miles per second (2 to 5 km/sec), and they only travel through rock, not liquid. They move in a motion similar to the way the end of a rope moves when you shake it. When S waves move through rock, they cause the molecules in the rock to jiggle up and down or back and forth. The molecules move against each other and pass the jiggle movement along. After the S wave has moved through them, they fall back into the position they had been in before the S wave came along.

When S waves reach water, they simply stop. The reason for this is that the molecules that make up water are spaced further apart from each other than the ones that make up rock, and they can move around more freely. Because of this, molecules in water are less likely to hit against each other. They do not resist the S wave, so it is not passed along through them.

Surface waves

The there are also two kinds of surface waves, known as "Rayleigh waves" and "Love waves." They travel along the surface of the earth away from the epicenter of the earthquake. Surface waves move much slower than body waves and may last as much as five times longer.

Rayleigh waves

Once the waves are in the earth's surface, they are known as "Rayleigh waves," which move the same as waves in the sea move. Rayleigh waves move molecules in a circular motion.

Love waves

Love waves are also waves that have made it to the earth's surface. They move with a side-to-side motion and thus cause rock molecules to shake from side to side. The sideways movement of Love waves can cause a lot of damage to buildings as they yank away foundations.

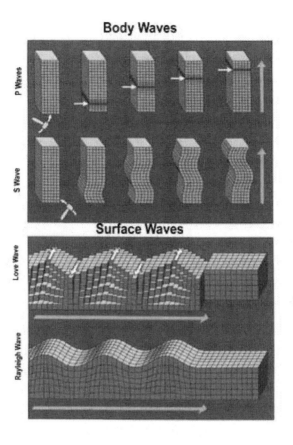

Types of seismic waves.
Image credit: USGS

Foreshocks and Aftershocks

"Foreshocks" and "aftershocks" are tremors felt before or after the main earthquake. Foreshocks may warn of the earthquake, and aftershocks may cause further damage. Since foreshocks occur before an earthquake strikes, they can be used, in some cases, to predict the possibility of an earthquake. We will talk more about this later. Aftershocks occur after a major earthquake as the rock shifts and settles into place. They can occur from several hours to several months after the first quake. These tremors are much smaller than the first earthquake, but may cause further damage to already damaged buildings and roadways.

Landslides, Avalanches and Mudslides

Aftershocks may also trigger other catastrophic events, such as avalanches, landslides and mudslides. This usually happens in areas where there are mountains. Large amounts of snow, rock or mud may come loose as the ground shakes and then slide down the side of the mountain. These events move extremely fast with tremendous force, crushing everything in their path, including trees, buildings and crops. Avalanches, landslides and mudslides can even destroy entire cities.

Vibrations from an earthquake and its aftershocks can cause weakening in the soil and rocks in surrounding cliffs, which may lead to an event known as a "landslide." One of the worst landslides to occur due to an earthquake happened in Gansu, China, on December 16, 1920. The residents had made their homes in the cliffs, and when the earth shifted, over 180,000 people were killed after the vibrations shifted the soil and their homes collapsed.

On August 17, 1959, an earthquake occurred near West Yellowstone, Montana, that caused a landscape that then created a lake. This happened after the earthquake loosened the rock in the wall of Madison Canyon, which was located approximately 19 mile (30 km) west of West Yellowstone. The loose rock fell into the Madison River and created a damn. The lake that was created as a result is known as "Earthquake Lake." It is 200 feet (60 m) deep in some places.

Epicenter

The point on the earth's surface that is located directly above the center of the earthquake, or its focus, is called the "epicenter." This is the location where the shaking is the strongest. It is directly above the place where the fault shifts. Sometimes an actual earthquake on the surface of the earth can occur miles from the quake's epicenter, however, because the fault is long and damage can spread. For instance, Mexico City suffered a serious earthquake in 1985, but the epicenter of the quake was 220 miles (350 kilometers) away, on the Pacific coast.

Pinpointing

An earthquake's epicenter can be "pinpointed," or located, by scientists known as "seismologists" who study seismic activity. They use various tools, which we will talk more about later, that measure the seismic waves of an earthquake and create a "seismogram" (an image of the created by the data gathered about the waves). Seismologists work in centers worldwide to gather information about seismic waves. They gather this data for many reasons, including being able to determine the origin of an earthquake.

When an earthquake is reported, seismologists hurry to compare the data they have gathered in an effort to figure out the exact location of the earthquake's epicenter. They do this by looking at the information gathered from different points in the world. Since a seismograph cannot tell seismologists the direction the seismic waves came from – it can only tell them how far away the waves came – sets of data from three locations are required to be able pinpoint where the waves originated. In order to pinpoint the epicenter, seismologists at each location first examine their seismogram and determine how far away the waves began. They then draw a circle around their location with a radius equal to the distance the waves traveled. The place where the circles from three (or more) seismic stations overlap is the location of the earthquake's epicenter.

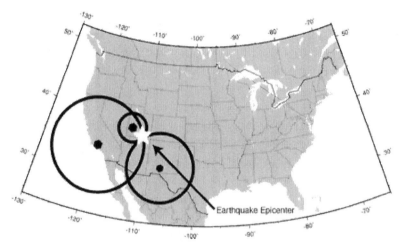

Pinpointing the epicenter.
Image credit: USGS

Chapter 3: Measuring an Earthquake

Seismograms

Seismologists use instruments called "seismographs" to gather information about ground movement before, during and after an earthquake. Seismographs make lines on graphs, called "seismograms," which show the earthquake's strength. A seismograph keeps a continuous record of the ground's movement. It records north-south, east-west, or up-and-down motions. This then provides a comprehensive record of the earth's motion. There are two kinds of seismographs. One kind of seismograph measures side-to-side, or "horizontal," motion. The other kind measures up-and-down, or "vertical," motion.

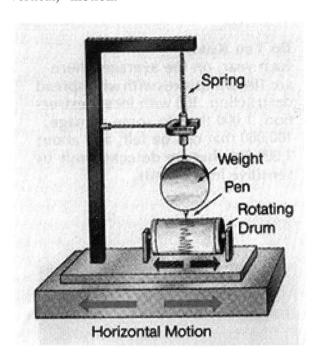

Seismographs are made up of several parts. They have weights attached to a wire or spring that senses movement. They have a device that is able to translate seismic waves into a form that can be recorded. And they have an instrument, such as an ink pen, to record the information. A rotating drum holds a roll of paper on which information is recorded. The weight, since it is hung by a wire or spring, stays still during an earthquake. The rest of the instrument moves when the earth moves. As the drum moves, it rubs against the pen, and the movement of the earth is recorded on the paper as squiggly lines. This recorded information is known as a "seismogram." It gives a record of when an earthquake occurred, how long it lasted, and when the seismic waves reached the seismograph. It also reveals how strong the earthquake was.

Some seismographs use electronic instruments to record the earth's vibrations on photographic paper or on magnetic tape. These records are played on instruments that actually allow you to hear the sound of the earthquake's seismic waves. More advanced seismographs are attached to computers, and the movement of the earth appears on the screen of the computer monitor as squiggly lines.

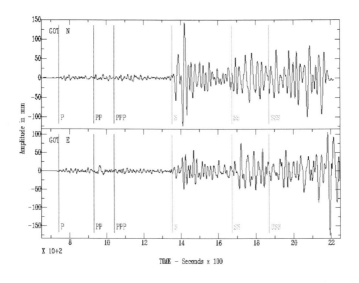

Seismograph.
Image credit: USGS

Richter Scale

The strength of an earthquake can be measured as a number on a scale. The most popular scale is the Richter scale, which was developed by Charles Richter in 1935. The Richter scale measures the strength of an earthquake on a scale of 1 to 10. Each increase of one on the Richter scale means a 10x increase in the strength of an earthquake. So, for instance, an earthquake that measure a magnitude 4 on the scale is 10 times stronger than an earthquake that measures a 3 on the scale.

There is no upper limit to the Richter scale, but the largest quakes on the scale have had a magnitude of approximately 8.9. Earthquakes of this magnitude are rare and highly unlikely. Most rock seems to reach a certain limit where it snaps and releases energy before being able to build up enough energy to cause a magnitude 10 earthquake.

Geologists have found in recent years that the Richter scale does not always measure the magnitude of an earthquake accurately. While news reports still give the Richter scale measurement, seismologists now use more precise magnitude scales. Currently, the magnitude scale known as the "moment magnitude scale" is in use. This scale is based on the strength of the rock in the area where the earthquake occurred, how much of the earth's surface area was broken during the quake, and the distance the rock slipped along the fault. This information can be determined by modern seismographs. The actual length and depth of the break is also taken into consideration. The numbers of the moment magnitude scale increase at a rate of 10, the same what is used for the Richter scale.

Modified Mercalli (MM) Intensity Scale

While seismographs provide information about where the earthquake originated and reveal information about its seismic waves and the Richter scale measures the strength of the earthquake on a numerical scale, another way to measure an earthquake is by observations of the people who were present when the earthquake struck to determine how severe it was. This is the concept at the heart of the Modified Mercalli (MM) Intensity Scale. Originally invented by Giuseppe Mercalli in 1902 and modified in 1931 by American seismologists Harry Wood and Frank Neumann, the MM Scale measures the "intensity" of an earthquake. An earthquake's intensity is the effect it has on the earth. Instead of having a mathematical basis like the Richter scale, the MM Scale is a random ranking based on observation of an earthquake's effects. It measures how much an earthquake shakes objects and the damage it causes to buildings.

Gathering information about the kinds of damage people saw and what they felt helps provide an accurate picture of the strength of the earthquake. It also helps to compare what people in different locations experienced during an earthquake. While people in one location may have only felt mild shaking and experienced hanging object swinging, those in another location may report dishes breaking and small objects moving. Assembling these observations help seismologists determine the scope of an earthquake.

Based on a series of 12 responses that people have to the effect of an earthquake, the observations on the scale range from the earthquake going completely unnoticed by anyone on the lower end to complete destruction on the upper end. In between these two extremes are a number of possible responses, such as "felt by nearly everyone" and "some dishes, windows broken" to "damage great in poorly built structures" and "heavy furniture overturned." The main difference between the Richter scale and the Mercalli scale is that the Richter scale measures how big an earthquake is – it clearly measures an earthquake's size – while the MM Scale measures how bad it was – it measures the damage done by the earthquake. The two scales combined provide a complete and accurate assessment of how large an earthquake is and how much destruction it caused.

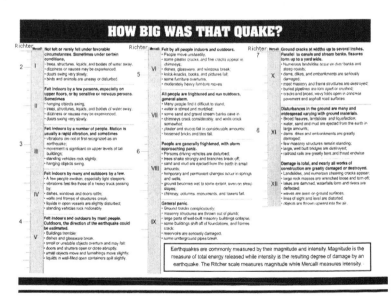

Gathering these kind of observations is a mammoth task. Most countries have agencies assigned to do the work. In the United States, for instance, the job is performed by the United States Geological Survey's National Earthquake Information Center. They mail questionnaires to police and fire departments and to volunteers in the area where an earthquake occurred. This information is then used to draw a "map" of the scope of an earthquake. The map gives a clear picture of how much damage the earthquake caused over a broad area.

Chapter 4: Predicting Earthquakes

Although there are patterns in the way earthquakes occur, earthquakes often seem to occur randomly. They seem to hit without warning. This can be frustrating, and scientists are actively trying to figure out if there is a pattern to the events that lead up to an earthquake.

Much information can be gained by studying the history of a particular fault. Doing this can reveal patterns that can help seismologists to detect a way of predicting earthquakes in the future for the area surrounding the fault. This might include estimating years during which an earthquake may occur as well as how likely it is one will happen. Although predicting the exact day, month and year an earthquake may occur is difficult, seismologists have had luck in predicting the likelihood of an earthquake occurring within a range of years in a specific area in recent years.

Another way seismologists can predict future earthquakes in an area is to see if there has been an increase in seismic activity. They are looking for "foreshocks," the unusually small earthquakes that can occur from mere seconds to many weeks before a major earthquake.

Scientists also try to predict earthquakes by using equipment that measures movement in the earth's rocks. One way they do this is to place special equipment in areas known to be at high risk for earthquakes. For instance, "strainmeters" and "creepmeters" are instruments that can measure tiny movements along fault lines. They can help to measure how much the rock along a fault has changed. A strainmeter measures how much a rock has been bent or twisted by stress. "Tiltmeters" can show any changes in the way the ground slopes. They measure the tilt of the rock by checking its elevation in relation to the fault. These devices are useful for helping to warn people about the potential of a big tremor occurring.

Another method scientists are using to predict tremors is by measuring groundwater levels in wells in areas that are susceptible to earthquakes. They place special equipment in the wells that transmits data to a central seismographic station. Sudden changes in the level of groundwater could mean that the ground is moving.

All of this information can help geologists to determine the likelihood of an earthquake occurring in the area in the future. It is, however, not extremely reliable: sometimes foreshocks and tilt and strain mean that an earthquake will soon follow, and sometimes they don't. Still, as geologists gather the information and study the patterns over a period of time, they gain a better understanding of the chance of an earthquake happening.

They are always working to find better ways to be able to predict when and where earthquakes will occur. By doing this, they can warn people about earthquakes sooner, which could help to prevent the loss of lives and injury. When they are warned in advance, people are able to take steps to stay safe during an earthquake. The information scientists have gathered can help in some cases, but in many cases, they just don't know when an earthquake might strike. This is why it is essential to always be prepared.

Animal Behavior

An earthquake can sometimes be predicted by observing the behavior of animals in an area. Animals often give warning signs since they are able to sense movement in the earth better than humans. Some animals may become restless or try to leave the area right before an earthquake hits. Domestic animals, such as horses, cattle, goats and dogs, are often reported as having been restless before a major earthquake hits. Zoo staff member have reported observing the same sort of activity in wild animals in confinement; the animals may pace and try to leave their enclosures directly before an earthquake occurs. This may be because they can feel the shaking of the earth when the shock waves are still deep under the earth's surface.

Wildlife, such as rabbits and rats, have been observed moving to higher ground, perhaps in an effort to get away from the vibrations they are sensing through the earth's surface. Most of the observations of animal behavior are noted and recalled after the earthquake strikes; many people don't heed the changes in animal behavior because they could be caused by many factors.

Chapter 5: Damage

An earthquake can cause such minor damage that it goes almost unnoticed or it can cause considerable devastation that takes years to recover from. It all depends on the magnitude and strength of the earthquake. Minor damage includes some items being knocked off of shelves and hung pictures falling off of walls, but no damage to buildings. Medium damage includes slight damage to buildings, such as cracks in walls or foundations. There may be few or no causalities due to damage. Major damage includes the collapse of buildings, bridges and roadways and colossal loss of lives. Other factors the scope of damage depends upon the are the depth of the earthquake, the epicenter location and population density.

Minor earthqauke damage to a home.

Photo credit: Adam DuBrowa/FEMA

Post Earthquake Damage

In addition to events caused by aftershocks, such as landslides, avalanches and mudslides, earthquakes can also trigger other disasters, including liquefaction, tsunamis and fires.

Liquefaction

When earthquakes occur near seacoasts and lakes, a process known as "liquefaction" can happen. It occurs within minutes after an earthquake strikes. The rock and soil along the area is "saturated," or mixed with water. This causes the soil to become weaker than when it was solid ground. This is due to water surrounding the grains of soil, which keeps them from being tightly packed together. As the earthquake's vibrations move the saturated soil, it becomes unsteady and can cause buildings on it to slip off of their foundations and collapse. The buildings may sink into the soil. Basically, the soil literally becomes "liquefied."

Tsunami

Another event that can occur after an earthquake is a "tsunami." Earthquakes can cause tsunamis when an earthquake occurs under the ocean and causes movement of the water, which creates the huge waves. A tsunami is a seismic sea wave that forms when the shift in the earth's tectonic plates causes a large displacement in ocean water. The word "tsunami" is the Japanese word for "large wave." A tsunami can travel across the ocean at speeds up to 500 miles per hour (750 km/hr) and can reach heights of 50 to 100 feet (15 to 30 m). When tsunamis hit land, devastation can occur. They flood the land, drowning people and destroying buildings and crops. Entire villages and cities can be wiped out. Most tsunamis occur in the Pacific Ocean.

Tsunami warning systems can alert scientists of the formation of potentially destructive tsunamis. When instruments that have been placed in the ocean detect a change in ocean water levels, an alert is issued to areas nearby. People who live in these areas are told to evacuate the coastal areas and move to higher ground. Similarly, when an earthquake occurs in an area, people are warned to be on the watch for tsunami activity.

Tsunamis can travel far from the epicenter of an earthquake. For instance, after a 9.5 magnitude earthquake struck Chile on May 22, 1960, a tsunami hit land on the shores of Hawaii approximately 15 hours after the earthquake, and then struck the Japanese islands of Honshu and Hokkaido seven hours later – more than 22 hours after the initial earthquake occurred! This event alerted scientists to the distance tsunamis can travel long after an initial quake happens. Now, tsunami warnings are issued over vast distances to warn people to evacuate coastal areas after an earthquake has occurred.

Fires

Fires often occur after an earthquake and can cause further damage. They are a result of gas or electrical lines snapping or bursting when the earth shifts. It is estimated that about 90 percent of the damage caused by the 1906 San Francisco earthquake was caused by fire.

Cleaning up

While an earthquake may last only a few seconds, the processing of cleaning up the damage afterward can take a long time. After a significant earthquake strikes, people may be trapped under buildings and need to be found and rescued. Injured people need treatment. If damage from an earthquake is extensive, the area will require help from outside. It may need supplies, such as food, water, medicine, blankets and shelter. It may need doctors and nurses. It may need search and rescue teams to help search for survivors.

Once people have been rescued and the injured have been treated, power and water lines will need to be repaired so that electric and water can be restored to the area. Homes and buildings will need to be repaired or rebuilt. Countries from all over the world may offer to help clean up an area after an earthquake, sending rescue workers, supplies and other forms of aid. For instance, after the 2011 earthquake and tsunami in Japan, nations from all over the world pitched in to help Japan, including Australia, New Zealand, South Korea, Germany, the United Kingdom and the United States.

Cleaning up Hachinohe 2011.
Photo credit: Thomas Ahern/US Navy

If an earthquake is minor, it will require less time and effort to clean up afterward. After checking that everyone is uninjured and accounted for, people check to see if any damage was done to property. They check to make sure utilities, such as gas and water, are still working. They examine their homes for damage, such as cracks in the walls or foundations. They look in their yards to see if any trees have been knocked over. They carefully open closets and cupboards to make sure nothing has been disturbed during the earthquake. If someone finds significant damage to their property, they will have to ask their insurance company for money to help pay for the repairs. Homeowners who live in earthquake zones should always have insurance to cover the possibility of any damage to their property.

Major property damage to home.
Photo credit: Andrea Booher/FEMA

Chapter 6: Notable Earthquakes in History

China, Shensi province, 1556

One of the deadliest earthquakes in history was the massive earthquake that struck Shensi province, China in 1556. It is estimated that approximately 830,000 people were killed. By modern estimates, the earthquake is thought to have been 7.9 or 8 on the Richter scale. It is considered one of the top four deadliest natural disasters in the history of the world.

Portugal, 1755

On November 1, 1755, a significant earthquake struck Lisbon, Portugal. Buildings collapsed, fires broke out and over 60,000 people died. The entire city was destroyed.

San Francisco, California, 1906

A substantial earthquake shook the city San Francisco for one full minute on April 18, 1906. Fires broke out after the earthquake that engulfed the city for days. More than 3,000 people were killed, and 28,000 buildings were destroyed.

Japan, 1923

One of the most destructive earthquakes in history happened in the cities of Tokyo and Yokphama in Japan on September 1, 1923. The ground shook for a full five minutes. More than 100,000 people died as buildings collapsed and fires broke out. It measured 8.2 on the Richter scale and destroyed approximately 575,000 homes.

Valdivia, Chile, 1960

One of the strongest earthquakes ever recorded hit the town of Valdivia, Chile in 1960. It measured 8.3 on the Richter scale and caused the town to sink almost 7 feet (2 meters)!

Anchorage, Alaska, 1964

A serious earthquake struck Anchorage, Alaska on March 27, 1964, causing the ground to shake for close to three minutes. Known as the "Great Good Friday Earthquake," the earthquake registered 9.2 on the Richter scale and X to XI on the modified Mercalli scale. It was the strongest earthquake to occur in 400 years. The quake started a landslide that then destroyed other nearby towns. 131 people were killed. At least 42 aftershocks were recorded the weekend the Great Good Friday Earthquake hit.

Good Friday Earthquake

Guatemala, 1976

On February 4, 1976, a major earthquake struck Guatemala at 3:01AM. Most people were sleeping when the quake occurred. Approximately 23,000 people died, and 76,000 were injured. Many of the adobe homes in the area could not withstand the earthquake and over a million people lost their homes.

China, Tangshan province, 1976

Another deadly earthquake struck in Tangshan province, China, on July 28, 1976. The earthquake measured 7.9 on the Richter scale. Approximately 650,000 people died, and 164,000 were injured. It is considered the largest earthquake of the 20th century in terms of death toll.

Mexico City, 1985

An earthquake with a magnitude of 8.1 struck Mexico City on September 19, 1985. It was precluded by a 5.2 foreshock on May 28, 1985 and followed by two aftershocks, one on September 20, 1985 with a magnitude of 7.5 and the second, with a magnitude of 7.0, seven months later on April 30,1986. The earthquake killed more than 7,000 people.

Russia, 1995

On May 28, 1995, an earthquake struck the island of Sakhalin, near Russia. It destroyed the town of Neftegorsk and killed approximately 2,000 people, almost two-thirds of the town's entire population. This earthquake is notable because it occurred in the plate boundary between the North American and Eurasian plates, which was previously believed to be inactive. The earthquake provided insights regarding plate movement for seismologists.

Kobe, Japan, 1995

A considerable earthquake hit Kobe, Japan on January 17, 1995. Known as "The 1995 Great Hanshin Earthquake," it killed more than 5, 500 people and damaged 190, 000 buildings. Its epicenter was 10 miles (16 kilometers) away from Kobe, and its focus was 10 miles (16 kilometers) beneath the ocean floor. More than 600 small aftershocks occurred within 48 hours after the main earthquake, causing further damage.

Chapter 7: Studying Earthquakes

By studying earthquakes, geologists gain information that is useful to helping them understand why earthquakes have occurred and how to prepare better for them in the future. The scientific study of earthquakes is known as "seismology," because it looks at the seismic activity of the earth. By using seismographs to gather information about seismic waves, scientists can learn not only learn about the natural occurrence of earthquakes in our planet, but also gain insight into how our own activities may trigger them, such as when earthquakes are triggered by explosions in mines or when the walls of man-made dams in waterways break.

The study of earthquakes dates all the way back to 132 A.D., with the invention of the first seismometer by the Chinese astronomer and mathematician Chang Heng. Today, people who want to study earthquakes for a living go to college to become seismologists. They take classes in physics, math, chemistry, geology and computer science to learn how to be a seismologist. Many go on to find jobs in the field, including working for government agencies or research institutes or for companies that engage in activities that require knowledge of seismic activity, such as mining companies. Others may teach at colleges or high schools.

Preventing Damage

We can't keep earthquakes from happening, but we can try to decrease the damage they cause. The main way to do this is to make buildings that will not easily collapse during an earthquake. They must be built so that they do not sink or fall over. If they are made to be able to sway, they can better resist an earthquake without breaking apart. For instance, buildings that are built on a solid base are more likely to be damaged during an earthquake. If the building is built on rubber springs, it can sway gently when an earthquake happens.

Seismologists work with engineers and planners to help design and build structures that are better able to withstand earthquakes. They have learned lessons from studying earthquakes worldwide. By observing the damage caused to buildings, they can better understand how to design buildings that can withstand some earthquake damage. There are many ways they do this. One way is to bolt buildings to solid foundations. Another way is to strengthen building walls with reinforced concrete or steel beams. Rubber and steel pads can be installed at the base of a building to help it resist minor earthquakes. These devises are called "isolators" and act like shock absorbers do in an automobile. They allow the building to be flexible and sway during an earthquake, which helps to decrease the possibility of damage during an earthquake. These methods are tested out with special vibrating machines using to scale models. These vibrating machines simulate the rumblings of earthquakes, and allow builders and seismologists to test out their designs before putting them into play with real buildings.

While these methods help to decrease damage to a building during an earthquake, there is no guarantee that these reinforced buildings will be able to stand up to a mighty big earthquake. However, these methods have been put into place in buildings where major earthquakes often occur. Japanese architects have developed specially-designed high-rise buildings in Tokyo, and San Francisco's tallest building – the TransAmerica Pyramid – stands 853 feet (260 meters) high and was designed to withstand earthquakes.

Elevated highways are also a concern to engineers who try to prevent the damage that may occur when an earthquake strikes. When the concrete columns that support these highways crumble and fall during an earthquake, the resulting damage and loss of lives can be devastating. One way in which engineers are working to prevent this is to design flexible columns that can withstand the impact of an earthquake. However, this strategy has not always been successful. The elevated Hanshin Expressway in Kobe, Japan was designed to tolerate a significant earthquake. But when the 1995 quake struck, some of its columns broke and part of the roadway flipped over. Engineers are currently trying to figure out ways to prevent this from happening again.

Safety

There are many ways to stay safe before, during and after an earthquake. The main things to have ready before an earthquake strikes are an earthquake emergency kit and a family communication plan.

If you live in an area where earthquakes occur, your home and office should be equipped with an earthquake survival kit. It should contain the supplies you will need to keep you alive after an earthquake. It should contain a flashlight and extra batteries, a portable radio and a first-aid kit. There should be enough water for each person, approximately a gallon of water per person for three to five days, and also enough food for three to five days, including such items as pasta, rice, jerky, energy bars, crackers and canned goods. Don't forget a can opener. Include personal hygiene items, such as toilet paper and towlettes, and heavy plastic bags for disposal of trash. Include a pair of sturdy shoes, a tarp and blankets. You also might want to include necessary tools, such as a fire extinguisher, wrenches, an ax, a hammer, a crowbar and rope. The items should be stored in a cool, dry place inside a large, sturdy container, such as a footlocker, construction bucket or trash barrel.

A "family communication plan" is a plan you make with your about what to do during and after an earthquake. You need to consider, for instance, how you will contact each other after the earthquake, since you may not be together in the same place when an earthquake strikes. Make up a contact card for adults in the family to keep in their wallets or purse and for children to keep in their book bags. It should include contact information of a family member or friend who lives outside of the area. This is the person every family member is to contact after an earthquake strikes to notify that they are safe.

In addition to these steps, there are other things you can do ahead of time to keep a home safe during an earthquake. These include making sure heavy items are not on high shelves, and that breakable items, such as glass and ceramic, are stored in cabinets that can be latched shut. Pictures and framed items should be securely attached to walls, and items that could fall during an earthquake should be braced. All heavy appliances should be strapped to a wall or bolted to the floor. Dangerous products, such as pesticides and flammable items, should be stored away securely. The main things to consider when earthquake-proofing your home is what could move and cause harm or damage when the ground begins to shake? Then take steps to make sure these items are secured or stored away.

Earthquake Drills

Schools located in earthquake zones have regular earthquake drills so students can practice what they are supposed to do during an earthquake. This includes learning how to "Drop, Cover and Hold On," an action recommended by people who study what to do during emergencies. If an earthquake happens, you are supposed to Drop down onto your hands and knees, Cover your head and neck under a sturdy table or desk and Hold on to the desk or table or table until the shaking stops. If there is no desk or table available, then you should crouch down by an inside wall and cover your neck and head with your hands.

School children practicing earthquake drill.

Photo credit: Jessica Robertson/USGS

It also helps to practice earthquake drills at home. Do this by identifying safe places in your home, such as sturdy tables or places against inside walls you can crouch during an earthquake. Move to these locations during drills so you get used to doing it, and also practice Drop, Cover and Hold.

What to Do During an Earthquake

If you are inside during an earthquake, you should stay there and Drop, Cover and Hold as soon as the ground starts to shake. Stay away from windows and doors and outside walls. Remain inside and do not try to go outside until the earthquake is over.

If you are outside when an earthquake strikes, you should move away from buildings, streetlights, utility wires and bridges. Once you are in the open, stay there until the shaking stops. Do not attempt to go inside a building.

If you are in a car when the earthquake happens, pull over somewhere as soon as you can that is not near bridges, trees, utility wires or overpasses. Stay in your car until the shaking stops.

If you end up being trapped under debris during an earthquake, take steps to remain safe and to let rescuers know you are there. Cover your mouth and avoid shouting – you don't want to inhale dust. Do not light a match because there could be something that could catch on fire nearby. Tap on a pipe or a wall if you are near one so people can hear where you are.

After an earthquake ends, the first thing you should do is to look around and make sure it is safe to move. If you are in a building, exit it. If you are not with your family, contact the person listed on your contact information card, so your family knows you are safe.

Conclusion

Like all natural disasters, earthquakes may cause people to feel a great deal of anxiety and fear. Since you don't know when one might strike, it is easy to always feel uneasy. However, this doesn't help anything. The best thing to do is to be prepared – have an earthquake emergency kit nearby wherever you are and have a plan. Check your home on a regular basis to make sure it is "earthquake ready" and practice Earthquake Drills so that you know what to do if an earthquake happens without having to stop and think about it. While it may be impossible to stop an earthquake from happening, information and awareness can help to save lives. Scientists are working every day to learn more about these powerful natural disasters in an effort to help us be safer in the future.

Bibliography

Kusky, Timothy M. *Earthquakes: Plate Tectonics and Earthquake Hazards*. Infobase Publishing, 2008.

Morris, Neil. *Earthquakes*. Crabtree Publishing Company, 1998.

Reger, James P. "Earthquakes and Maryland." Maryland Geological Survey website. http://www.mgs.md.gov/esic/brochures/earthquake.html

Rogers, Daniel. *Earthquakes*. Raintree Steck-Vaughn Publ., 1999.

Staff. "Preparing Your Earthquake Survival Kit." *Los Angeles Times* website. http://www.latimes.com/news/local/earthquakes/la-me-earthquake-checklist-g,0,3391133.graphic

"Earthquakes." FEMA website. http://www.ready.gov/earthquakes

"Earthquake Hazards Program." USGS website. http://earthquake.usgs.gov/earthquakes/

"How Are Earthquakes Studied?" Michigan Tech School of Geological and Mining Engineering Services website. http://www.geo.mtu.edu/UPSeis/studying.html

"Protect Yourself During an Earthquake...Drop, Cover, and Hold On!" Earthquake Country Info website. http://www.earthquakecountry.info/dropcoverholdon/

"Studying Earthquakes." Council for Geoscience website. http://www.geoscience.org.za/index.php?option=com_content&view=article&id=1628:studying-seismology&catid=141:seismology&Itemid=615

"The Modified Mercalli Scale." USGS website.
http://earthquake.usgs.gov/learn/topics/mercalli.php

"Where Earthquakes Occur." University of Berkeley California
Seismological Laboratory website.
http://seismo.berkeley.edu/blog/seismoblog.php/2008/09/29/where-
earthquakes-occur

The Science of Hurricanes

Introduction

Hurricanes are the most powerful storms on earth and can bring strong winds, heavy rain, and flooding. They can be terribly destructive. A strong hurricane can blow buildings apart and fill the air with flying debris. It can flood a coastal town to such a degree that residents are left stranded on rooftops awaiting boats that will rescue them.

The word "hurricane" comes from earlier civilizations that lived in the Tropics in ancient times. These violent storms were called "Hunracen" by the Mayan people of South and Central America and "Hurican" by the people of the Caribbeans. Both of these names referred to the angry god who was believed to be behind the terrible destruction caused by the storms. We know today that hurricanes are not created by an evil god but instead arise through a unique set of weather conditions.

The United States has about five hurricanes a year. In other parts of the world, they may happen year-round. Hurricane season in the United States beings in June and lasts through November. The months that the most number of hurricanes occur are August and September. Not all hurricanes strike land, but when they do, the amount of destruction can be considerable.

A hurricane at full strength can cause ocean waves to rise up 50 feet or higher and can deliver 6-12 inches of rain over an area in a second. It can have winds that may reach over 155 miles per hour and can last for days or even weeks. These winds are strong enough to uproot trees and tear roofs off of houses. Hurricanes are considered the worst type of storm and they can cause more damage and loss of life than any other type of weather event.

While some hurricanes may only last for a few hours, others last for days. Most hurricanes die out in less than a week. Some, however, can last much longer. For instance, in 1971 Hurricane Ginger stormed for 20 days and it took more than 11 days for the storm to finally fall apart.

As you can see, hurricanes carry the potential to cause devastating amount of damage and loss of life in a short span of time. What does a hurricane look like? How does it begin? What causes it to finally die out? Let's take a look at the factors behind these tremendously powerful forces of nature.

Chapter 1: What Is a Hurricane?

A hurricane is a whopping. intense and spinning storm with unusually strong winds that develops over an ocean. The winds of the storm circle around a center are referred to as the "eye" of the hurricane. The storms form in warm areas around the equator. Warm water temperatures feed the storm and cause it to grow larger and stronger. Although hurricanes often start as unusually small storms, they can eventually reach sustained winds that may exceed 199 kph (74 mph). They can be 200 to 600 miles wide and rise 40,000 to 50,000 feet into the sky.

What does it Look Like?

When viewed from space, a hurricane forms the shape of a spiral. This is due to the clouds that have formed around its center. It looks terribly much like a donut, with the storm's "eye" being the donut's hole.

View of Hurricane Andrew from above. Credit: NOAA

Chapter 2: Physical structure

Eye and center

The "eye" of the hurricane is the center of the storm. It has only light winds and a few clouds and is the calmest place of the storm. This occurs because a cloud-free space is created as the warm air in the center pushes against the storm's thunderclouds, causing them to wrap around it. Winds are thus not able to extend into the area, and the eye is simply filled with light breezes and clear skies. The eye may be large or small, depending on the speed of the hurricane's winds. Stronger winds will wrap around the eye tightly and cause it to be small. As the winds weaken, the eye expands. An average eye will be about 20 miles wide. Although the shape of some hurricane eyes are round, they are generally oval in shape.

When the eye of a hurricane passes over an area, people are sometimes fooled into thinking the storm has passed. However, once the eye passes over, the storm returns with the same violence as before.

Eye wall

Around the eye of the hurricane is a barrier known as the "eye wall." This is where the most violent winds and the heaviest rains take place. The winds can blast at speeds of 150 mph or more. They can stir up tremendous waves when they are over the ocean or uproot trees and destroy buildings when they are over land. The eye wall carries billions of tons of water that have risen up out of the sea that fall back down in the form of rain. The eye wall can tower as high as 50,000 feet into the sky and can be 30 to 150 miles in width. From outside, it looks like a wall of dark clouds randomly lit by flashes of lightning. At the top of the eye wall, air pushes outward and then falls downward (spinning in a counterclockwise direction in the Northern Hemisphere and a clockwise direction in the Southern Hemisphere).

Hurricane Katrina eyewall. Credit: NOAA, by pilot Dewie Floyd.

Chapter 3: Where and When Do Hurricanes Occur?

Hurricanes form in the tropic areas along the earth's equator when the oceans are at their warmest temperatures and the air above the water becomes heavy with moisture. This period is known as "hurricane season." Over the western Pacific, hurricane season lasts from June through October. In the Atlantic and along the Gulf coasts, it runs from June through November. However, hurricanes can form anytime the water temperature rises above 80 degrees and the air is filled with moisture.

Hurricanes that affect the United States most often begin in the Gulf of Mexico or the Caribbean Sea. Some, however, may begin as far away as the Cape Verde Islands, which is off the coast of West Africa. Early September is the height of hurricane season for the United States.

How Does a Hurricane Begin?

In order for a hurricane to form, three factors must be present: the waters over which the storm forms must be above 80 degrees F, the air over the waters must be filled with moisture, and winds must be blowing in from different directions and joining together.

The hurricane begins first as a "tropical disturbance" (an area of enhanced cumulonimbus activity with no wind circulation to move them). If the conditions noted in the above paragraph are present, the tropical disturbance may eventually develop into a "tropical cyclone" (a storm system that is characterized by a large low pressure center and numerous thunderstorms that produce strong winds). Tropical cyclones begin in the warm, moist atmosphere over tropical ocean waters. Moisture evaporates from these warm waters and enters the atmosphere. As it rises, cooler air from above drops to take its place. As the warm air continues to rise, the air pressure drops and the winds blow faster. A phenomenon known as "the Coriolis effect" may cause the air to spiral inward. This causes the air to heat even more, and the winds will then rise higher and spin faster. Bands of thunderclouds may begin to form from the moisture. All of this creates the perfect conditions for thunderstorms to form, and rain will fall in sheets. Within a few days, a powerful storm can develop from this cycle. As long as the temperatures of the ocean waters remains above 80 degrees and the winds continue to rotate, the storm will grow in size and strength.

When the wind speeds of the tropical cyclone exceed 25 mph, it is then officially classified as a "tropical depression." Tropical depressions are identified by numbers. For instance, it may be referred to as "Tropical Depression Three" (TD3). Once wind speeds reach 39-73 mph, the tropical depression will be upgraded to a classification of "tropical storm," and it may be given a name taken from lists originated by the National Hurricane Center. The list contains 21 common male and female names. The storm may be called, for instance, Tropical Storm Andrew.

Once a tropical cyclone reaches sustained wind speeds of 74 mph, it is officially classified as a "hurricane" if it forms in the North Atlantic, Caribbean Sea, Gulf of Mexico, or the west coast of Mexico. (If it forms in the North Pacific it is called a "typhoon", and if it forms in the Indian Ocean, it is called a "cyclone.") Thus, Tropical Storm Andrew becomes Hurricane Andrew. A "major hurricane" will reach wind speeds of 111 mph or higher. Hurricane Andrew, which struck the eastern United States coast line during the 1992 hurricane season, reached wind speeds of 115 mph.

Hurricane Movement: Trade Winds and Doldrums

Hurricanes are pushed westward by east-to-west winds known as "Tropical Easterlies," or "Trade Winds." These winds occur at 0-30 degrees latitude (along the equator) and blow approximately 10 to 15 miles per hour. If the winds move at higher speeds than this, the storm may move too quickly to be able to gain strength and may weaken and fall apart.

The easterly trade winds of both the northern and southern hemispheres meet at an area near the equator called the "Intertropical Convergence Zone" (sometimes referred to as the "doldrums" or "ITCZ"). As the air piles up near the surface of the ocean due to the converging winds, it forces the warm, humid air over the tropical oceans to rise. As the air rises, it cools and water vapor condenses into clouds and rain. This creates a narrow band of clouds and thunderstorms that encircle portions of the globe. If conditions are favorable, some of the thunderstorms that form along the ITCZ can develop into hurricanes.

The path of motion of a hurricane is sometimes referred to as its "track." No two hurricanes follow the same path. Its direction is determined by air currents and high and low pressure systems. Hurricanes may move in a straight line or their path may curve like a fishhook. Some hurricane paths will loop around. Often, a hurricane's path is unpredictable.

Chapter 4: Storm Clouds

Clouds, in general, form as humid air rises, evaporates, and cools causing the water vapor within it to condense into droplets. Storm clouds form when the humid air is heated from below, which causes it to rise to extraordinary heights, and when heat is also moving through the air vertically, causing the air to be "unstable." Storm clouds will build in height depending on the strength of the movement of the vertical air—the stronger the vertical movement is, the taller the clouds will become. The storm clouds that form in the unstable air are called "cumuliform." They can produce rain showers, which can sometimes be extremely heavy.

Classification

"Low-level" clouds can produce precipitation. The base of the cloud is between sea level and 1.2 miles high. Low-level clouds include "Stratus," a featureless cloud that forms as a sheet and that may produce fine drizzle; "Stratocumulus," which is featureless like Straus but broken into fluffy masses and may also produce fine drizzle; "Cumulus," which are white, fluffy clouds with flat bases; and "Cumulonimbus," which is a form of Cumulus that towers to a considerable height and may produce thunderstorms and hail.

"Medium-level" clouds have a base that is 1.2 to 4 or 5 miles above sea level in tropical regions and 1.2 to 2.5 above sea level in Polar Regions. Medium-level clouds include "Altocumulus," which are rolls of clouds joined together to form a sheet; "Altostratus," which are pale, featureless clouds that form a sheet; and "Nimbostratus," which is a featureless cloud that forms a large sheet and that may produce rain or snow.

"High-level" clouds have a base the is 3 to 11 miles above sea level in tropical regions and 2 to 5 miles above sea level in polar regions. High-level clouds consists entirely of ice crystals. These include "Cirrus," which are patches of stringy clouds that are sometimes swept into strands; "Cirrocumulus," which are patches of thin clouds that form a ripple-like pattern; and "Cirrostratus," which are thin, nearly transparent clouds that form into a sheet.

Latent heat and dew point

"Latent heat" is the heat required to change a solid (such as ice) into a liquid (such as water) or gas (such as water vapor) without a change of temperature. When latent heat is released by freezing or condensation (when water collects as droplets on a cold surface), the surroundings become warmer. This is an important concept to understand when considering how storm clouds that can produce hurricanes are formed. As warm air rises, the water vapor in it condenses. This makes the air warm even more, and thus, the air rises higher. Warm air holds more water vapor than cold air. And if moist air is cooled, the water vapor in it condenses into droplets. The temperature at which this happens is referred to as the "dew point." Air at dew point temperature contains a lot of water vapor. The amount of water vapor in the air is known as its "relative humidity."

Evaporation, Condensation and Cloud Formation

Water vapor condenses when relative humidity is 78% or lower if the air contains particles of soluble substances (substances that dissolve in water), such as salt crystals. If the air contains particles of substances that don't dissolve in water, such as dust, water vapor then condenses when relative humidity is about 100%.

Water vapor condenses on particles knows as "cloud condensation nuclei" (CCN). The water droplets vary in size depending on the size of the nuclei they condense on, but gradually grow in size as they evaporate and lose water as they are warmed by latent heat during condensation. As they grow in size, a cloud is formed.

Chapter 5: Convection and Low Pressure

Hadley cells

The pattern of movement for air moving between the equator and the tropics is called a "Hadley cell." It is part of a three-cell model of atmospheric circulation that explains how warm air moves away from the equator and is carried into high latitudes while cold air moves towards the equator. It also explains how pressure systems in air are distributed. For instance, whenever air is rising, the surface pressure will be low, and when air is descending, the surface pressure will be high. In mid-latitudes, where polar and tropical air meet, pressure is variable due to the movement of the rising and falling air.

The definition of a Hadley cell was developed as scientists tried to explain why trade winds blow regularly enough that European sailors could come to rely on them. The winds are highly dependable in both strength and direction. In 1686, Edmund Halley, an English astronomer, offered the explanation that, since the air at the equator is heated more than air in any other location, when it rises and cold air flows in near the surface from either side to replace it, trade winds are formed. However, he had no explanation for why the trade winds blow northeast and southeast, instead of due south and north, which is the direction in which they would blow if his theory were correct.

In 1735, George Hadley, an English meteorologist, suggested a modification of Halley's theory. While Hadley agreed that the air at the equator warms more strongly than anywhere else and that it is replaced at the surface when it rises, he proposed that the rotation of the Earth from west to east swings the moving air, causing it to blow from the northeast to the southeast instead of due north and south.

While he was correct that the rising air was swinging, and changing direction, the reasons he gave for it doing so were incorrect. In 1856, William Ferrel, an American meteorologist, claimed the swing was due to the tendency of the rising air to rotate about its own axis.

Hadley had also suggested a reason for why heat is moved away from the equator and this explanation was correct. He said that the warm air near the equator moves to a considerable height all the way to both of the poles, where it descends. In the same way that vertical movement that is driven from below in a *fluid* is called a "convection cell," the similar cell in the *air* that Hadley defined is labeled as a "Hadley cell."

Due to the rotation of the earth, it is not possible for a single, large Hadley cell to form. Instead, the warm air near the equator rises to a height of approximately 10 miles, then, as it moves away from the equator, it cools and descends to a latitude that is between 25 degrees North and 30 degrees South. These areas are defined as separate Hadley cells. When Hadley cells reach the tropics, part of the air flows towards the equator and the rest flows away from it. Meanwhile, cold air descends over the poles and flows away from them at a low altitude. Somewhere around 50 degrees latitude, it meets up with the warm air flowing away from the Hadley cells near the equator. When these two kinds of air meet, it is called the "polar front." The air rises again when it is at the polar front. Some of it flows toward the pole, where it joins a high-latitude cell, and the rest flows toward the equator, where is joins with the Hadley cell. Warm air moves away from the equator, and cool air moves toward it in this complicated cell system. This air movement can cause instability, which can create the conditions that give rise to the tropical storms that may eventually turn into hurricanes.

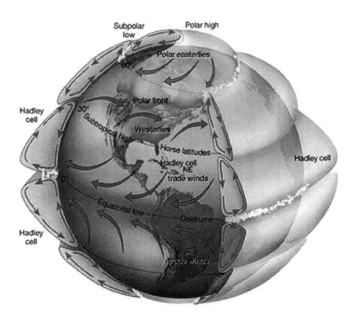

3-D Hadley cell diagram. Credit: NASA

Air pressure

The air in wind, like everything else in the universe, is made up of tiny particles called "atoms." These atoms are joined together in clusters that are called "molecules." When air warms, the molecules move faster and spread apart, and the air becomes lighter and rises. When air cools, the molecules move slower and press together, and the air becomes heavier and sinks. When air is cool, its pressure (the force at which it pushes against things) is high. When air is warm, its pressure is low. Air pressure can be measured with an instrument called a "barometer."

The amount of sunlight in an area can influence whether air will warm or cool. The warm or cool air will gather in the area in a large mass that can be thousands of miles wide and several miles high. These masses are known as high or low pressure systems and will determine the type of weather in the area. Specifically, a high pressure system creates mild weather and a low pressure system can create conditions that are ideal for storms. Air moves between a high pressure system and a low pressure system as wind. If the difference in temperatures between a high pressure system and a low pressure system is large, the wind can become immensely strong.

Vortices

You may be familiar with whirlpools in water. They demonstrate the way moving water is affected by "vorticity," which is the tendency of a moving fluid to begin turning about an "axis," (an imaginary line). It then creates a "vortex" (a whirlpool). Vorticity begins when two streams of air or water flow side by side but at different speeds. The one that is moving faster is slowed down by the slow-moving one and begins to curve toward it. When air moves in this way, vorticity makes it curve until it moves in a circle. If the circle becomes smaller, "angular momentum" (the quality that causes a spinning circle to continue to spin) will cause the air to move faster. In a hurricane, this means that the air that is spiraling inward toward the eye will increase in speed. This is what makes the winds around the eye of the hurricane so fierce. The "Coriolis effect," which will be explained next, is what determines the direction in which the winds blow.

The Coriolis effect

The Coriolis effect is a force created by the Earth's rotation that causes winds to curve. It occurs all over the earth but most notably near the Earth's equator, in the area known as the tropics. It is here that the sun's rays are at their strongest, and they warm the air and cause it to rise. The rising air in the tropics then moves south or north toward the poles of the earth. At the same time, cool air from the poles is moving into the area. These masses of air do not move in a straight line because of the rotation of the earth. Since the earth is turning faster than the air masses are moving, it causes them to change direction and curve sideways. This curving is known as the "Coriolis effect." Winds moving north and south can curve so much that they end up coming from the west or east. It is named after the French physicist Gaspard de Coriolis, who was the first scientist to describe the force.

The Coriolis effect also influences the direction in which the masses of high pressure air and low pressure air move. For instance, south of the equator, air in a high pressure system moves in a counterclockwise direction and air in a low pressure system spins in a clockwise direction. North of the equator, the opposite is true, with air in a high pressure system moving in a clockwise direction and air in a low pressure system moving counterclockwise.

Chapter 6: What Happens Inside a Hurricane

As air moves in from the areas of higher atmospheric pressure surrounding a storm to fill the deepening tropical depression, it begins to rotate. As it does, a noticeable structure will form. It is this structure that maintains the force of the storm as it moves from tropical depression to tropical storm to hurricane. This creates an enormous amount of energy.

As the Coriolis effect curves air around the low pressure area, it is opposed by friction between the wind and the sea. This causes the wind to slow down and weakens the Coriolis effect and makes the wind spiral inward toward the low pressure area of the storm. As the air spirals inward, it is warmed by contact with the ocean's surface. This causes it to rise. The friction present also causes spray to rise from the ocean's surface, which then evaporates and adds to the amount of moisture in the storm. All of this causes the air to become moist to a great height. As the rising air then cools, the moisture in it begins to condense. This then releases heat, which causes the air to rise higher. This creates cumulonimbus clouds to form that can rise to heights of up to 50,000 feet. These storm clouds then produce thunderstorms with heavy rainfall and hail.

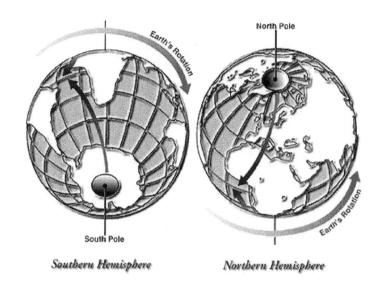

Diagram of Coriolis effect. Credit: NASA

As the wind speeds decrease near the top of the structure, the air begins to move slower than the earth's rotation and the Coroilis effect causes them to move clockwise so that they form curving lines of clouds. This creates the spiral effect of the hurricane. While some of the air disperses at this point, some of it tends to sink. It moves to the center of the vortex, warming as it descends. Its increased temperature allows it to be able to hold more moisture. It becomes clear and still, forming the eye of the hurricane.

However, in the upper and middle parts of the storm structure, the difference in temperature is vast, especially in comparison to the eye of the storm. This causes a vast difference in air pressure. This difference in air pressure increases the energy of the storm. The eye of the hurricane has the lowest air pressure. This reduced pressure allows the surface of the sea to rise, creating a storm surge. The storm surge is a tremendously destructive element of a hurricane, and we will talk about it in greater detail in the following section.

Chapter 7: Hurricane Damage

Saffir/Simpson Hurricane Scale

A hurricane is classified by the strength of its winds. The Saffir–Simpson Hurricane Scale (SSHS) classifies hurricanes into five categories distinguished by the intensities of their sustained winds.

Category 1: Hurricanes classified as Category 1 storms are the least intense storms. Wind speeds are between 74-95 mph. The winds can be dangerous and may cause slight damage to mobile homes and may uproot or damage trees and shrubbery. An example of a Category 1 hurricane is Hurricane Humberto, which developed over the Gulf of Mexico and stuck High Island, Texas in 2007.

Category 2: Hurricanes classified as Category 2 storms have wind speeds of 96 to 116 mph. The extremely strong winds may cause moderate damage to houses and can blow over unanchored mobile homes. Trees may be uprooted. Roads may flood. An example of a Category 2 hurricane is Hurricane Floyd, which hit North Carolina in 1999.

Category 3: Hurricanes classified as Category 3 storms have wind speeds of 111 to 130 mph. The winds can do extensive damage. Trees may be snapped or blown down, and small buildings and mobile homes may be badly damaged. Hurricane Ivan, which hit Gulf Shores, Alabama in 2004, is an example of a Category 3 hurricane.

Category 4: Hurricanes classified as Category 4 hurricanes have wind speeds of 131 to 155 miles per hour. The winds can cause complete destruction of mobile homes and extensive damage to other buildings. An example of a Category 4 hurricane is Hurricane Opal, which struck the Florida panhandle in 1995.

Category 5: Hurricanes classified as Category 5 hurricanes have winds greater than 155 miles per hour. They can cause catastrophic damage, including major flooding and complete destruction of buildings. Hurricane Camille, which hit the east coast in 1969 and caused flooding in Mississippi, Louisiana, and Virginia, is an example of a Category 5 hurricane.

Pine trees snapped by force of wind of Hurricane Andrew, a category 5 hurricance. Credit: NOAA photo library

Kinetic energy and wind force

Just as every object in motion carries a certain amount of energy, known as its kinetic energy, so does a hurricane contain kinetic energy. The amount of kinetic energy in a hurricane will determine how powerful it is. The amount of energy per cubic meter of storm can be calculated using a formula that multiplies half of the density of the air by the speed of the air cubed. Forecasters use this number to figure out how destructive a hurricane is going to be. It is a better gauge for measuring the raw destructive power of a storm that the Saffir/Simpson Hurricane Scale, which only measures the strength of the storm's winds.

Storm Surge

A "storm surge" is a wall of ocean water that is approximately 50 to 100 miles wide. It rises as a result of a hurricane and overflows onto the land. It is considered to be the most destructive force of a hurricane. A storm surge sweeps along the coastline when the hurricane hits land. It floods coastal towns and cities and also pushes excess water into bays, rivers, and creeks, causing them to overflow.

Storm surge pushing water ashore during hurrican. Credit: NOAA photo library

A storm surge is created when the hurricane is still over the ocean. High pressure pushes down the water that surrounds the eye while the water directly under the eye rises, since that's where the pressure is at its lowest. This creates the dome of water that can cause so much destruction when it strikes land. The lower the pressure is in the eye, the greater the surge.

A "storm tide" is a storm surge and a regular "high tide" (the point at which the ocean tide is at its highest) combined. The two together create considerable water heights that can create extreme flooding. During the worst hurricanes, storm tides can flood streets to depths of 15 feet or higher. These depths, combined with high wind speeds, can cause extensive damage.

Flooding along the Texas coast following passage of Hurricane Beulah. Credit: NOAA photo library

How Hurricane Damage is Predicted

Many organizations, including the U.S. National Oceanic and Atmospheric Administration (NOAA), maintain weather watching satellites. NOAA's GOES-8 satellite, for instance, is positioned over the Atlantic Ocean. It is always gathering and transmitting images of the weather systems below it. Another satellite, GOES-10, is situated above the Pacific Ocean and performs the same duties. These satellites allow meteorologists to keep track of the conditions that may lead to a hurricane, and enable them to follow a hurricane once it forms. The technology for these satellites was introduced in the 1960s. Before that, many hurricanes went undetected, and damage from the storms was considerable. Thanks to satellites, however, it is impossible for a developing hurricane to go unnoticed. They are the most indispensable device currently available for monitoring hurricanes.

Hurricane Andrew - visible image from METEOSAT 3 Andrew was approaching the Florida coast.

Credit: NOAA photo library

Other organizations besides NOAA also play a part in tracking hurricanes. When a tropical storm develops in the Atlantic Ocean, the Caribbean Sea, or the Gulf of Mexico, for instance, scientists at the National Hurricane Center in Coral Gables, Florida go on alert and keep an eye on storm developments. They pinpoint the location of the storm using instruments such as weather satellites—which can observe Earth's weather from space—and weather balloons, which are equipped with measuring instruments and launched twice a day worldwide. The instruments help scientists to spot changes in temperature and the amount of water vapor in the atmosphere.

Watches and Warnings

Watches and warnings are used to alert people on land if a hurricane is headed in their direction. A "watch" is issued if an area appears to be threatened by a hurricane. If a hurricane looks as if it will strike land, a "hurricane warning" is issued 24 hours in advance. Forecasters issue watches and warnings to enable people to prepare in advance. For instance, if a hurricane warning is issued, residents board up homes and office buildings, close down businesses, and evacuate the area. This helps to prevent damage from the storms. Advance warning can also help to save lives. For example, in 1900—before forecasting was common—the Galveston, Texas hurricane killed over 6,000 people. In comparison, when Hurricane Andrew struck in 1992, only 26 lives were lost due to advance warning.

Chapter 8: How Hurricanes are Named and Tracked

When a tropical disturbance develops into a tropical storm, it is given a name so that it can be easily tracked. The name is taken from a list of 21 common male and female names. There are six lists of names, and they are rotated. A different list will be used each year for six years. Once all of the names have all been used, scientists begin again with the first list. If a storm causes extensive damage, its name is retired. It is removed from the list and will no longer be used. Examples of names that are no longer in use include Katrina (2005), Andrew (1992), and Hugo (1989).

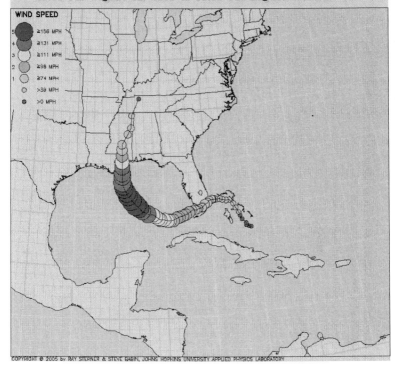

NOAA image of Hurricane Katrina tracking map. Credit: NOAA

Once a tropical storm has been named, pilots known as "hurricane hunters" take on the work of tracking it. These pilots fly four-engine planes that are stationed at the United States Air Force base near Biloxi, Mississippi or at Miami International Airport. The pilots and crew members on these planes are trained to gather information on hurricanes using the equipment on board the planes. When a tropical storm develops, they fly through the wall of the storm to the eye. Once there, they circle the eye and plot its location and the speed of the wind. Using a device known as a "dropsonde," they can measure air pressure, temperature, and humidity. The dropsonde is a metal cylinder that is attached to a small parachute. The crew members toss it out of the plane so that it falls toward the ocean. The information gathered by the dropsonde is used by the scientists at the National Hurricane Center to forecast where the storm is headed. The scientists also use images from satellites and reports from ships at sea to track the storm.

Cockpit of plane used to photograph Katrina eyewall. Credit: NOAA, by pilot Dewie Floyd.

Chapter 9: Worst Hurricanes in U.S. History

Property Damage

The worst hurricanes to hit the U.S. in terms of property damage include Hurricane Katrina of 2005, a Category 3 hurricane with property damages of over $81 billion; Hurricane Andrew of 1992, a Category 5 hurricane with property damages of over $48 billion; and Hurricane Wilma of 2003, a Category 3 hurricane with property damages of over $21 billion. As you can see, a hurricane does not have to have a high category in order to be extremely destructive. Two of the most destructive hurricanes in the history of the U.S. were only Category 3 hurricanes.

Lives Lost

The worst hurricanes to hit the U.S. in terms of lives lost include the Great Galveston Hurricane of 1900, a Category 4 hurricane that took 8,000 - 12,000 lives; the Okeechobee Hurricane of 1928, a Category 4 hurricane that took 2,500 - 3,000 lives; and Hurricane Katrina of 2005, a Category 3 hurricane that took over 1,500 lives. Advancements in forecasting and tracking hurricanes has reduced the loss of lives due to the storms over the years.

Highest Recorded Windspeeds

Hurricanes that had the highest recorded wind speeds when they struck land in the U.S. are Hurricane Camille, which had wind speeds of approximately 190 miles per hour when it hit the Mississippi coast in 1969; Hurricane Andrew, with wind speeds estimated at 167 miles per mile when it moved over Florida in 1992; and the 1935 Labor Day Hurricane, which had estimated wind speeds of 161 miles per hour when it made landfall in the Florida Keys.

The Top 10

Hurricane Katrina of 2005

One of the most devastating hurricanes in the history of the U.S., Hurricane Katrina. With over $81 billion in damage, it is also one of the deadliest hurricanes, with over 1,500 lives lost. It is particularly notable for the damage it caused New Orleans, which actually avoided the worst of the storm's strength. This is due in large part to the high storm surge the hurricane created and to the fact that New Orleans is below sea level. The hurricane breached the city's levees, which resulted in extensive flooding throughout the city and its eastern suburbs. The storm began in the Bahamas as a tropical wave that emerged from the remnants of Tropical Depression Ten, which had been in the Caribbean. It gradually grew in strength prior to making landfall in Florida. It then crossed over southern Florida and emerged again over the water in the Gulf of Mexico over the Florida Keys, where it grew further in strength and then struck land in Buras, Louisiana and next near Bay St. Louis, Mississippi. Thus far, it is the costliest hurricane in U.S. history.

Hurricane Andrew of 1992

Hurricane Andrew made landfall in southern Florida on August 24, 1992, bringing with it a 17 foot storm surge. It created an 8 foot storm surge when it struck Louisiana two days later. With wind speeds of 165 miles per hour, it was classified as a Category 5 hurricane and is considered one of the most powerful storms in U.S. history. The storm began as a tropical wave that emerged from the west coast of Africa. This then became a tropical depression that eventually developed into Hurricane Andrew.

Hurricane Wilma of 2003

Hurricane Wilma struck Cape Romano, Florida on October 24, 2003 as a Category 3 hurricane. Considered the third costliest hurricane in United States history, it caused widespread damage estimated at $16.8 billion. Twenty-two deaths have been directly attributed to Wilma. The hurricane not only caused severe damage in southern Florida, but also in northeastern Yucatan, including Cancun and Cozumel. It also produced significant floods in western Cuba, where waves as high as 45 feet came over the sea wall into the capital of Havana. Swells as high as 50 feet were also reported. Hurricane Wilma is known for its record low barometric pressure of 882mb. At one point, the hurricane had an eye that was 2 to 4 miles wide.

The Great Galveston Hurricane of 1900

The Great Galveston Hurricane does not have a name because it occurred before the naming system for storms was established. The hurricane hit the Texas coast south of Galveston on September 8, 1900 as a Category 4 hurricane. It is considered the deadliest hurricane in the history of the United States, with an estimated 8,000 to 12,000 deaths. The high death toll was caused by combination of lack of warning (there were no accurate hurricane warning systems in place at the time), complacency (a number of storms had hit the area previously with no significant consequences), and the hurricane's high storm surge (8 to 15 feet). Damage to property was estimated to be $30 million, which is an unusually high amount for the time period.

The Okeechobee Hurricane of 1928

Considered the second deadliest hurricane in the history of the United States, the Okeechobee Hurricane had an estimated death toll of 2,500 and caused approximately $25 million dollars in damage. Most of the deaths were a result of a lake surge of 6 to 9 feet that flooded the areas surrounding Lake Okeechobee, the largest freshwater lake in Florida. The storm was first detected over the Atlantic on September 12, 1928. It then made its way through the Leeward Islands, hit land in Puerto Rico on September 13 as a category 4 hurricane. It then worked its way through the Bahamas and hit land near Palm Beach, Florida on September 16. It traveled over the Florida Peninsula on September 17 and struck North Carolina on the 19th. The hurricane had a central pressure of 27.43 inches, making it one of the top five hurricanes with that intensity to strike the United States.

Hurricane Hugo of 1989

Hurricane Hugo was the most damagine hurricane in the history of weather for its time. With winds reaching 160 mph, Hurricane Hugo was a category 4 hurricane when it made landfall just north of Charleston, South Carolina on September 22nd. The storm caused over 17 billion dollars in damage and took the lives of 56 people.

Hurricane Camille of 1969

Hurricane Camille was a category 5 hurricane that hit the gulf areas of Louisiana, Alabama, and Mississippi in 1969. The storm first made landfall in Gulfport, Mississippi on August 17, 1969 with a storm surge of 24.3 feet and estimated winds of 190 mph. All wind-recording instruments in the area were destroyed when Camille made landfall.
It then weakened and crossed Mississippi into western Tennessee and Kentucky, finally turning eastward across West Virginia and Virginia. With a minimum pressure of 26.84 inches, Camille is one of the top five hurricanes on record to hit the United States. Hurricane Camille left 250 people dead and caused approximately $1.421 billion dollars in damage.

The 1935 Labor Day Hurricane

Although the 1935 Labor Day Hurricane was an exceptionally small storm, it was immensely powerful. The Category 5 hurricane hit the Florida Keys on September 2nd. The storm's winds were estimated to be over 161 mile per hour, and it had a pressure of 26.35 inches, making it one of the most intense hurricanes to hit the United States. Due to the lack of wind measurement instruments at the time it struck, the wind speed is estimated against hurricanes that had similar pressure reading at landfall. The storm was responsible for 408 deaths in the Florida Keys, and its damage in the United States was estimated to be approximately $6 million.

Hurricane Charley 2004

Hurricane Charley, the most devastating hurricane to hit Florida since Hurricane Andrew in August 1992, was also the second costliest hurricane in the United States behind Andrew. The hurricanes's highest wind speeds were 145 mph, making it a Category 4 hurricane. Although Charley was a violent storm, it was small, and this kept its storm surge small. The surge was not estimated to be more than 7 feet. Still, the storm caused substantial damage, devastating Punta Gorda and Port Charlotte. Hurricane Charley left at least 15 people dead and caused $14 billion dollars in damage.

Hurricane Ivan 2004

Hurricane Ivan made landfall in the United States near Gulf Shores, Alabama on September 16, 2004 as a Category 3 Hurricane with 130 mph winds. It had formed at Cape Verde and rapidly developed into a Category 4 hurricane. It briefly weakened to a Category 2 before regaining strength as it moved through the extreme Southern Windward Islands of Barbados and Grenada, where it destroyed a large percentage of the buildings on the island of Grenada. It then reached Category 5 status before eventually weakening again. Ivan caused approximatey124 deaths throughout the Caribbean and the United States and $14.2 billion dollars worth of damage.

Conclusion

Studying Hurricanes

Scientists and researchers use many methods to study hurricanes, including sending planes equipped with unique instruments into a tropical storm or hurricane to measure the storm's structure, environment, and changes in intensity, using laser technology and computer animation to help understand how tropical storms form and evolve, and observing them from above via unmanned aircraft. By studying hurricanes, researchers can learn useful information that may help save lives and property in the future. For instance, they may be able to discover better ways to predict storms that can increase warning time and allow people to evacuate sooner.

Many organizations that study storms and weather, including NASA, the National Oceanic and Atmospheric Administration (NOAA), and The International Hurricane Research Center, currently have several hurricane research and projects underway. Following are some examples:

The International Hurricane Research Center's Windstorm Simulation and Modeling Project. This three-year project has four main research tasks. These include gathering high-resolution elevation data via airborne Light Detection And Ranging (LIDAR), an emerging technology that can provide topographic data, in participating South Florida counties. Accurate topographic information helps to predict storm surge flooding and damage; evaluating "storm surge models," which are 2-D and 3-D hydrodynamic models that help researchers study storm surges; computer stimulation and visualization of hurricane impacts; and developing public awareness and educational programs.

NASA Global Hawk research. NASA's Hurricane and Severe Storm Sentinel (HS3) program is currently assigning two of its Global Hawks to fly above hurricanes to gather data. Global Hawks are high-altitude, long-duration unmanned aircraft that can fly at altitudes greater than 60,000 feet for up to 28 hours. One of the Global Hawks is sampling storm environments and the other is measuring information such as rainband winds and precipitation. The goal of the mission is to gather data that will help researchers better understand storm intensity and how hurricanes form.

NOAA Hurricane Research Division Hurricane Field Program. The Hurricane Research Division conducts a field program that uses NOAA aircraft to collect and process data about hurricanes. Each year, the program includes several experiments that are part of the Intensity Forecasting EXperiment (IFEX). IFEX was developed in partnership with NOAA's Environmental Modeling Center (EMC) and its Hurricane Center (NHC). Its goal is to improve our understanding and prediction of hurricane intensity and to develop ways to better predict hurricanes. Experiments underway for 2012 include the GALE UAS Eye/Eyewall Module, which will focus on The interaction between the ocean and the hurricane; the NESDIS Ocean Winds Hurricane Experiment, which will aim to study the ocean surface wind field in relation to hurricane development; and TC-Ocean Interaction Experiment, which will address the role of the ocean and air-sea interaction in relation to hurricane intensity.

NOAA's Joint Hurricane Testbed. This program, which brings together the new technology, research results, and observational advances of many organizations, including the United States Weather Research Program (USWRP), its sponsoring agencies, the academic community and other groups, currently has several projects underway. All of these programs strive to improve, develop, and enhance current technology and observational tools used to gather information about all aspects of hurricanes. For example, a past project focused on developing unified dropsonde quality assurance. A dropsonde is a tool that is dropped from a plane to gather information about the eye of a hurricane.

Hurricane Safety

When a hurricane threatens an area, precautions need to be taken regardless of whether it is a Category 1 or Category 5 hurricane. You should take steps to protect your property and life. Since hurricane warnings are issued 24 hours in advance of the storm, you have ample time to take precautions before the storm makes landfall. If an evacuation order is issued, try to get an early start to avoid traffic jams on the roadways. A significant evacuation will clog the roadways. People who wait until the last minute to leave their homes may be stuck in traffic as the storm approaches.

If you do not have to leave the area, take steps to decrease damage to your property. Put objects that can be blown by high winds in a safe spot, such as bicycles, lawn furniture, and potted plants. Trim dead branches off of trees and bushes. Prepare your property for high winds by boarding up windows so that objects blown by wind will not break the glass. Purchase bottled water or fill containers with enough drinking water to last for at least a week. It is a good idea to fill bathtubs and sinks with water in case the local water supply becomes contaminated during the storm. Place any pets that live outdoors in a space where they will be safe, and provide them with plenty of food and drinking water. Make sure you have a flashlight, an emergency first-aid kit, a battery-powered radio, food that can be eaten without cooking, necessary prescription medications, and a blanket for everyone in the household on hand. Place all valuables in watertight containers and store them in the highest level of your building. You should unplug small appliances and turn off propane tanks.

When the storm arrives, stay indoors. Do not go outside until it has passed over. Once it has passed, be careful to avoid downed power poles and live wires when you go outside. Also be aware of dangling tree branches or other objects that may have been disturbed by the high winds.

If you live in a mobile home or an area that is below sea level and prone to extreme flooding, consider taking going to an emergency storm shelter. These are usually set up by the local Red Cross chapters and are located in sturdy structures that have ample bathroom facilities, such as high school gymnasiums. Go to a shelter as soon as an announcement is made that the space is open to ensure you get a place. Storm shelters fill up quickly. Make sure to bring food and clothing and bedding, such as an inflatable air mattress.

While hurricanes carry potential for devastating destruction, many factors can reduce the damage, including awareness and preparation as well as education and research. Understanding how hurricanes form and develop and knowing what steps to take when one strikes go a long way toward minimalizing the damage that may result from these storms.

Hurricane Image Links

Hadley cell diagram. NASA
http://serc.carleton.edu/details/images/10044.html

Coriolis effect diagram. NASA
http://sealevel.jpl.nasa.gov/overview/overviewclimate/overviewcl
imatemovement/

Hurricane Andrew overhead view. Nasa http://meso-
a.gsfc.nasa.gov/rsd/images/andrew.html

Hurricane Katrina eyewall. NOAA, by pilot Dewie Floyd
http://www.katrina.noaa.gov/eyewall/eyewall.html

Storm surge pushing water ashore during hurricane, NOAA photo
library http://www.photolib.noaa.gov/htmls/wea00402.htm

Cockpit of plane used to photograph Katrina eyewall. NOAA, by
pilot Dewie Floyd
http://www.katrina.noaa.gov/eyewall/eyewall.html

Hurricane Andrew - Pine trees snapped by force of wind at
Pinewoods Villa, NOAA photo library
http://www.photolib.noaa.gov/htmls/wea00536.htm

Flooding along the Texas coast following passage of Hurricane
Beulah, NOAA photo library
http://www.photolib.noaa.gov/htmls/wea00713.htm

Hurricane Andrew - visible image from METEOSAT 3 Andrew was
approaching the Florida coast, NOAA photo library
http://www.photolib.noaa.gov/htmls/wea00517.htm

NOAA image of Hurricane Katrina tracking map
http://www.ncdc.noaa.gov/special-reports/katrina.html

Hurricane Source List

Allaby, Michael. Hurricanes. Facts On File, Inc.: New York. 1997.

Florida International University: International Hurricane Research Center. Accessed 12-21-2012. **http://www.ihc.fiu.edu/**

Hirschmann, Kris. Hurricanes. Lucent Books: San Diego, California. 2002

NOAA Hurricane Research Division: FAQ Hurricanes, Typhoons, and Tropical Cyclones (website). Accessed 12-19-2012. **http://www.aoml.noaa.gov/hrd/tcfaq/tcfaqHED.html**

NOAA/National Hurricane Center website. Accessed 12-20-2012. **http://www.nhc.noaa.gov/**

Simon, Seymour. Hurricanes. HarperCollins Publishers: New York. 2003.

Souza, D.M. Hurricanes. Carolrhoda Books, Inc.: Minneapolis. 1996

The University of Illinois Department of Astmospheric Sciences (DAS): Movement of Hurricanes: Steered by the Global Winds (website). Accessed 12-18-2012. **http://ww2010.atmos.uiuc.edu/(Gh)/guides/mtr/hurr/mvmt.rxml**

The Science of Tsunamis

Introduction

While the sea brings life and livelihood to many people in the world, it can also bring unexpected disaster and destruction. Every year, Tsunamis strike. Every year, they bring devastation in their wake.

Tsunamis are powerful waves in the ocean that carry a massive destructive force. Tsunamis can snap trees in two, destroy houses, and toss ships and boats onto shore. They will wipe out everything in their path and flood large areas of land that is at a low level.

Tsunamis have been around for as long as humans have existed. Scientists and geologists have found evidence that reveals tsunamis have occurred worldwide throughout the history of the earth. Today, people living on islands in the Pacific, such as Hawaii, are most in danger of experiencing a tsunami.

The good news is that tsunamis do not occur particularly often. As few as five tsunamis are recorded every year, and only one of those is likely to be destructive. Some of the tsunamis that strike will only affect the general area where they originate while others may travel great distances in several directions, wiping out many cities and villages that are thousands of miles away from each other. It's hard to predict when a tsunami will occur and how strong it will be.

The word "tsunami" translates as "harbor wave" in Japanese. It is a combination of the Japanese word "tsu," which means "harbor," and "nami," which means "wave." Scientists may also refer to a tsunami as a "sea wave." A tsunami is a series of waves created by disturbances in a large body of water. The waves can be high – sometimes as high 70 or 80 feet! That's taller than many buildings! And while tides have nothing to do with the formation of tsunamis, if the tide is high when a tsunami forms, the tsunami may be more severe.

Tsunamis have the potential to cause a considerable amount of destruction in a short amount of time – a tsunami can kill tens of thousands of people in as little as 15 minutes! In light of this, scientists are always trying to learn more about these natural disasters in the hopes of creating accurate early warning systems in an effort to keep people safe.

Let's take a closer look at tsunamis and see what scientists have learned about them over the years.

Chapter 1: What is a Tsunami?

First of all, what is a tsunami? We know now that it is a wave, or series of wave, but what does it look like? What does it sound like? How and when does it form?

Technically, tsunamis are "seismic sea waves," which means that they are generated by the sudden displacement of water in the sea. The most common cause for the formation of a tsunami is the sudden displacement of the actual seafloor, which can occur due to natural disasters, such as earthquakes or landslides.

What does a tsunami look like? A tsunami does not look like the waves you might see at the beach. The waves of a tsunami do not break or curl. As a tsunami approaches the shore, it may appear to looking like a rapidly rising tide, or a series of breaking waves. The water approaches in rapid floods of water. Very violent tsunamis may appear as "bores," which are large, steep waves that look like a step-like wall of water. This kind of tsunami may have a churning, breaking front. Bores form when a tsunami moves rapidly from deep to shallow water.

Tsunami waves hitting shore.
Photo credit: FEMA

The water in a tsunami is usually brown in color, and the wave can reach up to 30 feet or more. It is high enough to crash down on coastal towns and the people who live in them. Viewed from the side, a tsunami resembles most waves you might see in the ocean – it may look like the letter "S" lying longwise. Viewed from above, a tsunami wave resembles a bull's-eye pattern of waves that spread out from a central point or groups of waves that are parallel that move in opposite directions. People who have witnessed a tsunami's approach describe it as looking like a great wall of water – ominous and high – coming at the shore.

Tsunamis look like a giant wave of water when they hit land.

The shape and height of a tsunami is determined by the shape of the ocean floor and the coastline where it strikes. Offshore reefs, which are strips of sand, rocks, or coral that rise from the ocean floor to the surface of the water, may break the force of a tsunami in some areas. Deep valleys, or cracks, in the seafloor may prevent tsunamis from growing too tall.

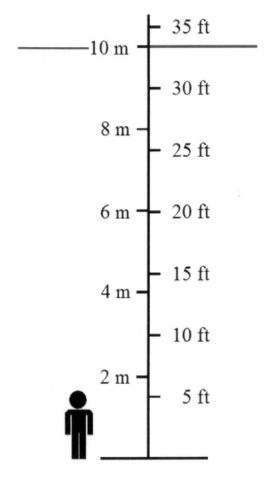

Tsunami size scale.

Survivors of tsunamis often describe the sound of them as they approach land being like a freight train. The sound of a tsunami's approach has also been likened to that of a jet airplane. It is a furious loud whoosh of a sound.

Tsunamis move extremely fast. They can travel at speeds of up to 700 miles per hour (805 km/hr) and can travel from one side of the Pacific Ocean to the other side in less than a day. Regular ocean waves generally only travel, at their fastest, about 50 miles per hour. Even though tsunami waves slow down when they hit the shore, due to the friction caused by the surface of the earth, they still travel approximately 40 miles an hour on land, which is why a human cannot outrun a tsunami wave. Although some people can run as fast as 30 miles an hour, most humans can only run between 5 to 15 miles an hour. This just isn't fast enough to outrun a tsunami!

When tsunami waves are in deep water, they measure less than three feet (.9 m) in height, but they can have lengths as great as 100 miles (161 km) from crest to crest (the "crest" of a wave is its highest part). When these masses of water surge to the surface, the waves spread, moving outward. While this can cause mass destruction when the waves reach land, the same event in the open ocean may go undetected. Because of this, tsunamis can be stealthy at sea. Waves that are capable of causing great destruction on land may pass more or less unnoticed in the open sea. They can even pass under a ship undetected!

By the time a tsunami wave strikes land, it has grown in height. The wave's height is known as its "amplitude." When a tsunami's waves have an amplitude of 130 or more, the occurrence is known as a "megatsunami." The strength and height of a tsunami depends on many factors, such as the shape of the ocean floor and the depth of the water. It depends on the amount and movement of the energy and force that caused it.

While the term "tidal wave" is often used to describe a destructive wall of water, it is not an accurate term for a tsunami. "Tides" are a natural occurrence, caused by the rising and lowering of ocean levels near the shoreline. These are caused by the gravitational pull of the moon. Tsunamis, on the other hand, are caused by violent actions in the earth, such as earthquakes, landslides, or volcanoes. A large meteorite landing in the ocean could also cause a tsunami. When the violent action of the earth displaces water in the ocean, tsunami waves form.

Now that we've established that tsunamis are technically waves and not tides, let's take a closer look at what a wave is, since this information will help us to better understand tsunamis, especially when we examine how the two differ from one another.

Waves

A "wave" is created when energy travels through the water. As it travels, it picks of water particles. The water particles move in circles as the energy of the wave passes through them.

All waves are comprised of parts. These include the "crest," which is the highest point of a wave, and the "trough," which is the lowest point of the wave. The distance from one crest to the next is the "wavelength." The time between one crest passing a point and the next crest passing the same point is called the "wave period." While an average ocean wave has a wavelength of approximately 500 feet (150 m) and a period of 10 seconds, tsunamis have long wavelengths and periods. The wavelength of a tsunami can be as long as 200 miles (322 km) and the period can be up to one hour.

How else do average ocean waves and tsunami waves differ? First of all, while most ocean waves are close to the surface of the ocean, a tsunami wave is different because it stretches all the way down to the ocean's floor in depth and for many miles in width. Most of the waves we see moving ocean water may look powerful, but they affect only the surface of the ocean, not the whole "water column" (which from the surface of the ocean down to the seafloor). Even when water on the surface is rough and choppy, the water in the ocean's depths is calm. But tsunami waves extend all the way down to the floor of the ocean and affect the entire water column.

Additionally, while average ocean waves slow and break as they near the shore, causing the front of the wave to become steeper than the back, tsunamis do not break. And while average ocean waves have white-foam crests at the top when they break, since tsunamis do not break, they generally do not have white crests.

We've noted that tsunamis and tidal waves are not the same thing. "Tidal wave" is a term used to define the rising and ebb of the ocean's levels. This happens gradually, over an extended period of time. You may have seen this if you have visited a beach. You may have noticed the water creeping up further and further on the sand, or, conversely, ebbing away more and more, revealing more sand. It is a steady cycle: the ocean level gets to its highest point (it rises) and then it ebbs away again (it lowers). This happens over and over again, regardless of the season or weather.

This rise and fall of the ocean is a series of long waves called "tides." They are so long they stretch from one side of the earth to the other. The interval of time between the highest tides and the lowest tides is approximately 12 hours. Tides are created by the pull of gravity between the Moon, the Earth, and the Sun. The Moon and the Sun pull on the ocean, causing the entire water body to rise and fall in a predictable manner. Tides are not like ocean waves; they rise and fall gradually, and they never crash onto a beach.

A tsunami wave is not dependent on the weather or the gravitational pull of the Earth, Moon, and Sun. A tsunami wave is a series of waves that only forms when there is a sudden and immense shift of the Earth's water due to a violent force.

The series of waves that makes up a tsunami is known as a "tsunami wave train." There are often no less than ten waves in a tsunami. Tsunamis waves have large distances between the individual crests of the waves. They move like other waves across the ocean, but they are different from other waves, because they have irregular wave train patterns that differ from normal ocean waves. While normal ocean waves have a more consistent wave train pattern, the wave train of a tsunami varies. Some tsunamis have a high initial peak followed by increasingly smaller waves, while others have the highest peak after a series of smaller waves. The reasons for this are dependent on the origin of the tsunami. For instance, a tsunami created by an impact to the water, which causes a sudden displacement, such as the impact of a meteorite, will result in an initial high peak wave. A tsunami created by an event such as an undersea volcanic explosion will have a series of smaller waves gradually increasing to larger waves. The wave train pattern is entirely dependent on the event that caused the tsunami.

Chapter 2: Science of Tsunami's

When an earthquake causes a tsunami, such as in the case of the 2004 south Asia tsunami, it is because two plates of the earth's crust grind together. In this case, it was the Burma plate and the Indian plate. These two particular plates are always grinding against one another. The Indian plate actually pulls the Burma plate down to a small degree, approximately 2.4 inches, every year. But on December 29, 2004, the stress that had built up on the Burma plate cause it to snap. It moved upwards, creating a split more than 600 miles (966 km) long. Some areas of the ocean floor were forced up as much as 50 feet (15 m). This sudden and immense movement displaced many gallons of water in the process, which then generates a tsunami. We will examine this process in closer detail in the following sections.

Causes

As we noted, tsunamis form when there is a sudden and violent displacement of water in the ocean. While earthquakes are the leading source of tsunamis, they can also be caused by volcanic eruptions and underwater events, such as landslides or nuclear explosions. Impact from outer space objects, such as asteroids, may sometimes cause tsunamis, but this is rare.

Plate Tectonics/Earthquakes

The violent action of an earthquake is the most common source of a tsunami. Earthquakes are caused by a sudden movement in "tectonic plates," which are the large plates of rock that form the earth's crust. These plates are what make up the ocean floor and the continents. They are rigid and do not break, bend or deform when they move, except along their edges. The plates move slowly – generally only about 1 to 2 inches (2.5 to 5.1 cm) a year. Occasionally, however, the force of one tectonic plate against another may cause greater movement. This sudden movement is what causes an earthquake.

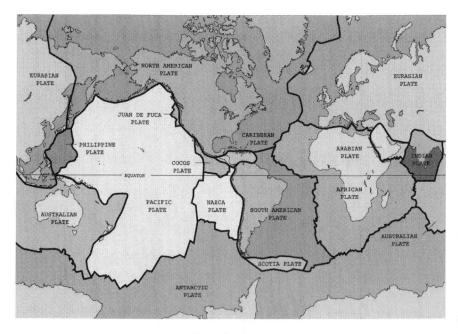

Tectonic plates.
Image credit: U.S. Geological Survey

To understand how this happens, it helps to look at the different types of tectonic plates. There are three types of tectonic plates. "Transform" plates are two plates that slide alongside each other, without moving away or toward one another. "Divergent" plates are plates that are slowly moving away from each other. "Convergent" plates, which move toward each other, are the type of plates may cause an earthquake. When convergent plates move toward each other, one plate may be forced under another. When this happens, it creates a "fault" (a crack in the Earth's crust). If one side of the fault slips to shift up or down suddenly, it causes an earthquake (a series of violent vibrations in the Earth's crust). When this happens, it can result in a sudden displacement of water in the ocean, which in turn can cause a tsunami.

While earthquakes every day, only a few move the ocean floor enough to create waves. This type of earthquake is generally powerful, measuring a 7.5 or higher on the Richter scale. An average of 20 earthquakes in this range occurs each year. Of these, only one or two of these may measure a magnitude of 8 or higher on the Richter scale. The rest of the earthquakes that occur either take place on land or are too far below the ocean floor to create a powerful enough disturbance to cause a tsunami.

Landslides

Landslides are the second most-common cause of tsunamis. A landslide happens when huge pieces of land fall into the water. This sometimes happens during earthquakes. The chunk of land may displace the water and create a tsunami when it falls into the water. This may not only occur when parts of land break off and fall in to the ocean, it may also occur when parts of land that are below the surface of the ocean breaks loose and slides deeper into the water. As it falls, the land pushes water ahead of it and sucks down the water that is behind it.

When a large mass of rock, sand, or mud falls into the ocean, it may create a tsunami if it moves fast enough. This is what happened with the tsunami that struck Lituya Bay in southeastern Alaska in 1958. An earthquake registering 8.0 on the Richter scale shook the area and caused part of a mountain to slide into the water, which in turn caused a tsunami.

Some storms may be capable of causing a submarine landslide that may result in a tsunami even if the storm waves do not reach the seafloor. This is because large storms can create a "storm surge," a mound of water in front of the storm that can reach heights of 20-32 feet (6-10 m). As the storm surge moves onto land, it is frequently preceded by a drop in air pressure, which may cause pressure changes on the seafloor. This is what may create a tsunami. An example of this is the tsunami event that happened in Japan in 1923. On September 1st, a typhoon raged across Tokyo, Japan, which was followed by a submarine landslide and earthquake that created a 36-foot (11 m) high tsunami that killed 143,000 in Tokyo.

The characteristic of tsunamis created by landslides depend on several factors, including the amount of material that moves during the landslide, the depth the material moves to, and the speed at which it moves.

Volcanoes

Volcanoes can also cause tsunamis. During the past 250 years, volcanoes caused approximately 90 tsunamis.

A volcano is an opening in the Earth's crust through which magma, the hot, liquid rock that is beneath the surface of the earth, and hot gases can escape. When the pressure of the gases and magma builds and forces through the opening, an eruption occurs. If the eruption happens underwater and is violent, it can release a lot of energy and create "shock waves," which can cause a tsunami to form. Some of the largest recorded tsunamis have been caused by volcanic eruptions.

Volcanoes can cause tsunamis when they erupt and send massive amounts of lava and rock into the ocean, either by direct flow or by falling into the ocean after flying through the sky. Approximately 20 percent of volcano-induced tsunamis happen when volcanic ash or pyroclastic flow (a dense, destructive mass of intensely hot ash, lava fragments, and gases ejected explosively from a volcano and typically flowing at great speeds) hit the ocean, displacing large amounts of water. An example of a tsunami caused by a volcanic eruption is the tsunami that happened in 1883 when the volcano at Krakatau erupted and formed a 130-foot (40 m) high tsunami that killed approximately 36, 500 people.

Volcanoes can also create tsunamis indirectly. For instance, when hot lava comes into contact with ocean water it may cause it to heat up so quickly that the water expands and creates a tsunami wave. Another way a volcano can cause a tsunami is to collapse and fall into itself after erupting. The water above it and around it may get sucked downward during the collapse, causing waves due to the sudden displacement.

Meteorites

Tsunamis can result when a meteorite, a large piece of rock from space that enters the Earth's atmosphere, strikes the surface of the ocean. It the meteorite is large enough, the force of the impact can create a tsunami. Although such an event has never been witnessed, scientists speculate that a meteorite may have struck the Earth and created a tsunami as recently as 3.5 billion years ago. Geologists also estimate that approximately 65 million years ago, an asteroid or comet plunged into the shallow sea in the area that is currently known as the Yucatan Peninsula in Mexico. The asteroid or comet is estimated to have been more than 6 miles (10 km) in diameter. When it struck the water, it created a "megatsunami" (a tsunami that has enough energy to travel to coastlines in many parts of the world) that spread around the world. It waves, estimated to be 150 to 300 feet (50 to 100 km) flooded the areas that are currently the southern states of the U.S. and Mexico. Geologists are able to make these estimates based on the evidence the tsunami left in its wake, including thick layers of rock composed of mud, sand, and broken rock fragments.

While this was a large object from space that fell into the ocean, even a smaller extraterrestrial object could create a significant tsunami wave that would result in flooding and damage.

Chapter 3: Where Tsunamis Strike

Most tsunamis occur along the shores of the Pacific Ocean. The areas that are at the highest risk for tsunamis include the coastal areas of Japan, the Phillipines, and the American west coast and Hawaii. The Pacific Ocean is the world's largest ocean, covering more than one third of the total surface area of our planet. The area that surrounds the Pacific Ocean is called "the Ring of Fire," which consists of many mountain chains and deep ocean trenches and is about 40,000km long. It runs from the tip of South America, up the coast of Chile, Peru, and Ecuador, through Central America and the west coast of Mexico, the United States and Canada. It extends to all the way to the southern coast of Alaska and along the Aleutian Islands, and then follows along the coast of Japan and the Philippines. It ends in New Zealand. Tsunamis may form anywhere along this horseshoe shaped rim.

Why is the Ring of Fire more likely to have tsunamis than other areas? The reason is because the area has more seismic and volcanic activity than other areas. Several of the Earth's tectonic plates push against each other in this region, creating ideal conditions for earthquakes and volcanic activity. Because of this, the Ring of Fire has 90% of the world's earthquakes and 75% of its volcanoes. Although approximately four out of every five tsunamis happen in this area, they also frequently occur in other areas, such as the Indian Ocean and the Mediterranean Sea.

The first places to be hit in the case of a tsunami caused by an earthquake are the towns and areas in close proximity to the earthquake's epicenter. A strong tsunami will be able to travel vast distances and strike areas far away from where it originates. For instance, the 2004 Indian Ocean tsunami first struck the communities near its epicenter in Sumatra and other nearby islands and then hit places further away, including India and Africa. Remember, a tsunami can travel fast – up to 700 miles per hour (805 km/hr) – and can travel across the Pacific Ocean in less than a day.

Development

As we have seen, the first thing that happens in the development of a tsunami is that a seismic event, such as an earthquake, occurs and sends "shock waves" outward. The initial waves of the tsunami are only a few feet high and travel fast. As the waves approach the coast, they travel through water that is shallower than it is further out at sea, and this causes the waves to decrease in speed while they are, at the same time, increasing in height. Keep in mind that as the wave slows down and increases in height, it is not losing any energy. While the waves display a reduction in wavelength, their frequency (the number of waves that pass a fixed point in unit time) remains constant. This process is known as the "shoaling" effect. By the time they strike the coast, the height of the waves combined with their frequency causes them to hit with deadly force. Tsunamis that strike the shore near the epicenter of an earthquake can reach heights of 100 feet (30 m) or more.

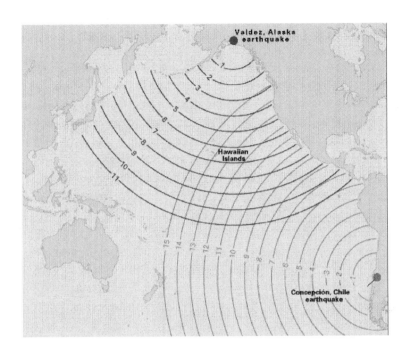

Travel times (in hours) are shown for the tsunamis produced by the 1960 Concepción, Chile, earthquake (purple curves) and by the 1964 Good Friday, Valdez (Anchorage), Alaska earthquake (red curves).
Image Credit: U.S. Geological Survey

The speed of a tsunami depends on gravity and the depth of the water. The deeper the water, the faster the wave. As the waves move into shallow water, they slow down. Since a single tsunami wave can be long, its front portion can be in shallow water while its rear portion is still in deep water. This means that the rear portion will move faster than the front portion. When this happens, the waves bunch up and get higher as the rear portion catches up to the front portion. Because the wave does not lose much energy as it moves onto land, this effect can cause a powerful tsunami, since the energy becomes concentrated in less water with higher waves.

Kinds of Tsunamis—Distant and Local

There are two kinds of tsunamis. "Distant" tsunamis are those that are created more than 600 miles (966 km) offshore. They are far enough away from land so that people have enough time to get to higher ground before they strike because scientists can predict them easier and give adequate warning. "Local" tsunamis, on the other hand, are much more dangerous. They are created somewhere between 60 miles (97 km) and 600 miles (988 km) from shore. They hit land within a very short time after forming – often within minutes. Because there is not enough time for a warning to be issued, these are the tsunamis that may take many lives. While landslides are often the cause of local tsunamis, they can also be caused by earthquakes. In some cases, a tsunami can be both distant and local. For instance, the Indian Ocean tsunami that occurred in 2004 was a local tsunami for communities in Sumatra and other nearby islands, but it was a distant tsunami for places farther away, such as India and Africa.

Another example of a distant tsunami is the powerful wave that was created when an earthquake shot through the ocean floor near the Kamchatka Peninsula of Russia in November, 1952. The resulting tsunami wave traveled across the Pacific Ocean and hit Japan, Hong Kong, Micronesia, Papua New Guinea, Kiribati, the Solomon Islands, Mexico, Guatemala, El Salvador, Costa Rica, Nicaragua, Ecuador, Chile, Peru, British Columbia, Washington, Alaska, Oregon, California, Hawaii, and New Zealand, all within a day!

Prediction

At the Pacific Tsunami Warning Center in Hawaii, scientists use seismometers to detect disturbances in the Earth's seismic activity. A seismometer records the movements of the earth, which can be used to detect earthquakes and measure their strength. It does this by detecting rumblings within the earth and measuring the vibrations inside of the Earth's crust. It then rates these vibrations on the Richter scale (a numerical scale that expresses the magnitude of an earthquake based on seismograph oscillations with values that fall between 0 and 9). Using these observations, scientists can foretell a tsunami, since tsunamis are often caused by earthquakes. For instance, when a tsunami hit the coastal towns in Indonesia, Sri Lanka, Thailand, and India on December 26, 2004, the center detected the earthquake that caused it in the Indian Ocean. It quickly sent out a warning of the possibility of a tsunami near the epicenter (the central point) of the earthquake. At first, they thought the earthquake was a magnitude 8.0 earthquake, which is strong but not catastrophic. But as more data emerged, they realized it was a serious earthquake. It turned out to be the most powerful earthquake the world had seen in over forty years! It measured 9.0 on the Richter scale, the highest value that can be assigned.

Scientists also use a combination of bottom pressure recorders and floating buoys to help predict tsunamis. A bottom pressure recorder is a device that measures the change in height of the water column by measuring associated changes in the water pressure. It measures the water pressure in the ocean every 15 minutes. By doing so, it can help to detect the passage of a tsunami since the pressure of the water on the seafloor is directly related to the sea-surface height. If the bottom pressure recorder picks up unusual activity, it will begin to measure the water pressure every 15 seconds to obtain more information.

Floating buoys are also an important tool that is used to help predict tsunamis. They work is combination with bottom pressure recorders. Floating buoys measure the conditions on the surface of the deep sea and send that data, as well as the data received via an acoustic link from the bottom pressure recorder, to a satellite. After the information is sent to the satellite, it will be transmitted to scientists at watch centers around the world. This system is known as DART (Deep-ocean Assessment and Reporting of Tsunamis) and plays a critical role in helping scientists to predict tsunamis.

DART surface buoy.

Sea level and tide gauges, which measure the sea level and tides at the shoreline, are also used to detect tsunamis. While they are primarily used for monitoring the tides for navigational purposes, tsunami warning centers also depend upon this data to observe the sea level and to determine whether tsunamis may have been generated during an earthquake. The gauges are located on piers in harbors along coastlines worldwide and send data in real time to tsunami watch centers. Many of these gauges use solar panels so that they will function even in the event of a power outage.

Other methods scientists use to guess where tsunamis may occur in the future include using historical records and generating computer programs to predict tsunamis. By looking at historical patterns of tsunami occurrence, for instance, scientists can create a database that may aid in predicting when in where tsunamis may occur in the future. Likewise, in the event of an earthquake, state-of-the-art computer programs can help to predict how long a tsunami triggered by the earthquake would take to reach places near its epicenter and beyond, even though there is not yet evidence a wave exists. This could help to provide accurate information to officials who may have only a few minutes in which to decide whether or not to sound an alarm. These sorts of computer-generated tools can be invaluable to scientists who are trying to forecast and predict when and where a tsunami might strike.

Chapter 4: Warning Signs

Some of the earliest warning signs can be observed and should be noted. Receding waters, for example, are a strong warning sign of the possibility of a tsunami. The water goes far out to sea, leaving a bare and naked beach behind. Many people may be deceived by this, and may even "play" on the beach that is bared as the ocean's waters recede, marveling at the pretty fish that are stranded and at the shells and other sea life left behind. They may try to "save" the fish and other sea life stranded on the rocks. Unbeknownst to them, however, the ocean's water has only briefly receded. It is about to return with a vengeance! The tides that have receded will soon come back in great quantity, and they will come back quickly. The best thing to do when you observe ocean water rapidly recede is to move to higher ground to a safe place as soon as possible.

When the water level along a seacoast rapidly drops like this suddenly right before a tsunami hits, it is known as a "drawback." It occurs rapidly and is caused by the valleys in between the waves of the tsunami. How does this happen? The best way to understand it is to consider that all waves have a "ridge" (which is high) and a "trough" (which is low). Either of these may be the first to arrive when a tsunami strikes. If the first part to hit is the ridge, observers will see a massive wave approaching. However, if the first part of the wave to strike is the "trough," the shoreline will recede and expose areas that are usually underwater. The sea will go out, leaving the ocean floor exposed. Fish and boats are stranded on the sand. Many people are curious when this happens and may walk out into the exposed sand to explore. But, as we've noted, this is an action that could cost them their life – soon after the waters drawback, the first wave of the tsunami will hit.

How much time does a person have to evacuate the area when a drawback occurs? To calculate this, consider that a typical wave period (or frequency) for a tsunami wave is approximately 12 minutes. This means that, during the drawback phase, the areas below sea level will be exposed after 3 minutes. Then, during the next 6 minutes, the trough will refill. In the next 6 minutes, the wave will change from a ridge to a trough again, causing the waters to drain again. This second drawback may sweep people who are on the exposed beach and debris out to sea. The process repeats when the next wave arrives.

What are other warning signs that a tsunami is about to happen? Some people theorize that animals can tell when a tsunami or earthquake is forming by sensing the geological changes in the earth. When a tsunami strikes, few animals seem to be caught off guard. There have been several reported instances of animals making their way to higher ground in the moments before a tsunami hits. For instance, witnesses reported elephants screaming and running for higher ground and flamingos abandoning their low-lying breeding ground just before the Indian Ocean tsunami made landfall. Dogs refused to go indoors, and zoo animals rushed into their shelters and would not come out. Experts suggest that the acute hearing and other senses animals have might make it possible for them to hear or feel the Earth's vibration and react. Very few animals die during tsunamis. They all make their way to higher ground.

Warning Systems

It is important to first distinguish the difference between a "Tsunami Watch" and a "Tsunami Warning." A "tsunami watch" means that there is a possibility of a tsunami and that people should be alert. A "tsunami warning" means that an actual tsunami may strike and that the area should be evacuated immediately. The Pacific Tsunami Warning Center automatically issues a Tsunami Watch for any earthquake magnitude 7.5 or larger (7.0 or larger in the Aleutian Islands) if the epicenter is in an area capable of generating a tsunami. They notify Civil Defense and provide the local media with public announcements. They then keep a close eye on tide gauge stations to see if a tsunami has been generated or not.

If the data reported by the stations confirms that a tsunami has been generated, a Tsunami Warning will be issued. A warning may be issued automatically if the system detects an earthquake powerful enough to create a tsunami nearby. The public will be alerted via the emergency broadcast system and evacuation will begin immediately.

Early warning systems, such as the DART (Deep-ocean Assessment and Reporting of Tsunamis) system mentioned earlier as a way of predicting tsunamis, also serves as a warning system for tsunamis. It is utilized by the Pacific Tsunami Warning Center system set up in the Pacific Ocean basin. Operated by the United States, this system allows for real-time tsunami detection to be made as waves travel across open ocean waters. It relies on buoys and equipment that measures water displacement and the pressure of sea waves to detect tsunamis. The equipment is highly sensitive to changes in vibrations in the earth and can alert people who live along the coasts of approaching tsunamis. After the data is transmitted via satellite to scientists, they will use it to warn the public via radio, television and sirens.

The Pacific Tsunami Warning Center was the first warning system to be put in place, but other similar warning systems now exist around the world, including The International Tsunami Warning System, which serves countries in or along the Pacific Ocean, including Australia, Canada, Chile, China, Guatemala, Indonesia, Japan, Mexico, the Philippines, and the United States, and the Japanese Tsunami Warning Service, which serves Japan.

While there was no warning system in place in the Indian Ocean before the tsunami struck in 2004, steps have since been taken since to establish one. The system is engineered to provide warning of approaching tsunamis to inhabitants of nations bordering the Indian Ocean. It includes a network of local communications that will help to spread warnings of approaching tsunamis (25 seismographic stations relaying information to 26 national tsunami information centers) and a monitoring system comprised of three deep-ocean sensors for predicting the possibility of a tsunami. The system became active in late June 2006.

The system was activated April 11, 2012 after a strong earthquake occurred off the west coast of Sumatra in Indonesia. It performed well overall during this first ocean-wide test, according to the Intergovernmental Oceanographic Commission of the United Nations Educational, Scientific and Cultural Organization (UNESC).

Chapter 5:Richter Scale

The Richter magnitude scale, frequently referred to as simply the Richter scale, was developed to as a mathematical device to compare the size of earthquakes and assign a single number to measure the energy released during an earthquake. It is used to measure the strength, or "magnitude," of earthquakes. The Richter scale is a "logarithmic" scale, which means that each step on it is about 10 times stronger than the one before it. For example, an earthquake measuring 5.0 is ten times greater in strength than an earthquake measuring 4.0.

The Richter scale was developed in 1935 by Charles Francis Richter at the California Institute of Technology. Although it was first intended for use only in a particular study area in California, it eventually became the standard tool used to measure earthquake magnitude worldwide. Scientists sue the Richter scale to determine whether an earthquake is strong enough to generate a tsunami.

Damage

A tsunami is devastating when it strikes – it can crush buildings, sweep away cars, and snap trees and utility poles in half. When a tsunami strikes, it sweeps away everything in it path. A tsunami's destructive power comes from its towering heights. The fast-moving massive wall of water can cause great destruction. It can sweep away entire towns and villages. Many of the people who survive a tsunami are left without homes to return to.

Debris left behind after tsunami.
Photo credit: U.S. Navy photo by Mass Communication Specialist 3rd Class Alexander Tidd

A tsunami can also take many lives. The tsunami that struck the coastal towns on the Indian Ocean in 2004 claimed 220, 000 lives. Tens of thousands of people were injured. The flooding that results may kill people, or they may be struck by debris during the flood. Tsunamis can travel up rivers and cause flooding far inland. The places that are in the most danger of being destroyed are those within 1 mile (1.6 km) of the shore and 50 feet (15 m) above sea level. The debris that travels in the flood can move at great speeds, killing or injuring those in its path.

As you can see, a tsunami can be one of the worst of natural disasters. The sheer power of the water in a tsunami wave is tremendous. Consider that a cubic foot of seawater weighs 64 pounds. There are millions of cubic feet of seawater in a tsunami wave! Additionally, the fast-moving waves behind the first wave of a tsunami catch up to it as it nears land and is slowed by friction. These waves add to the force and height of the first wave. But the first wave of a tsunami is not always the most powerful. Sometimes the waves behind it have just as much power, or more.

Tsunamis can also do other damage besides flooding. They can also spark fires when they hit land by splitting open containers filled with flammable liquids and gases, such as gasoline or oil. Oil-slicked ocean water in the tsunami can cause the flames to spread.

Tsunamis also often cause massive erosion – a process where water moves rock and dirt away from the ocean coast that normally takes place over a long period of time – in a brief period of time. A tsunami can strip a beach of its sand, and wash away soil and plants on the coastline. Damage to coastal cities and towns can be minimized by building sturdy sea walls and planting vegetation in the shallow waters along the shore.

Japanese coastline after withdrawal of tsunami.
Photo credit: NOAA/NGDC, Takaaki Uda, Public Works Research Institute, Japan.

Cleaning Up

After a tsunami strikes, there is much work to do in its aftermath. Organizations from around the world join together to do the immediate work of reuniting families, setting up temporary housing for those whose homes were destroyed in the tsunami, providing food and water, tending to the injured, and removing the dead. In the days and weeks following a tsunami, the main focus is on helping people to re-establish their lives after the disaster.

A Japanese search and rescue team searches the rubble near a high-rise building in Japan.
Photo credit: U.S. Navy photo by Mass Communication Specialist 3rd Class Alexander Tidd

After the dead have been buried and a daily routine has been put into place for the survivors, there is still much work to do. Entire communities must be rebuilt. This process can take several months, even years. Two years after a magnitude 9.0 earthquake struck Japan and generated a tsunami on March 11, 2011, work was still underway to rebuild the areas that were affected by it.

Chapter 6: Famous Tsunamis

8 Deadliest Tsunamis

1. Indian Ocean, 2004 (225,000 + deaths).
2. Crete-Santorini, Ancient Greece, 1410 B.C. (100,000 deaths).
3. Portugal-Morocco, 1755 (60,000 deaths).
4. South Sea China, 1782 (40,000 deaths)
5. Krakatau, Indonesia, 1883 (36,500 deaths).
6. Tokaido-Nankaido, Japan, 1707 (30,000 deaths).
7. Sanriku, Japan, 1896 (26, 360 deaths).
8. Northern Chile, 1868 (25, 674 deaths).

Notable Tsunamis in History

When the **Krakatoa** volcano, located in Southeast Asia on the Indonesian island of Rakata, erupted in **1883**, it birthed four tsunamis that spread and crashed into the shores of Java and Sumatra, located in the Sunda Strait. The waves reached heights of 131 feet (40 m) and killed approximately 40,000 people.

On April 1, 1946, a magnitude 7.8 earthquake struck the **Aleutian Islands** in Alaska. Five hours later, the tsunami this created hit Hilo, Hawaii. 159 people were killed, and the town was destroyed.

In 1958, an earthquake registering 8.0 on the Richter scale shook **Lituya Bay**, located in southeastern Alaska. The earthquake caused part of a mountain to slide into the water, which caused a tsunami. When the wave reached the opposite shore, it produced a water surge measuring 1, 722 feet (525 m), making it the largest tsunami ever recorded. Everything in the wave's path was stripped off of the mountain, leaving a barren area that can still be seen today.

On May 22, 1960, a magnitude 9.5 earthquake occurred off the coast of **Chile, South America**. It was the largest earthquake ever recorded. It created a series of deadly waves that spread across the Pacific Ocean. Within 15 minutes of the earthquake, walls of water hit along the coast of Chile, killing approximately 5,000 people. Fifteen hours later, the tsunami reached the Hawaiian Islands. Hardest hit was the Hawaiian city of Hilo. Its waterfront area was destroyed, and 61 people were killed. The tsunami hit Japan twenty-two hours later with a 20-foot (6 m) wave, killing approximately 200 people.

People run from an approaching tsunami in Hilo, Hawaii on 1 April 1946.
Image credit: Pacific Tsunami Museum in Hilo, Hawaii

On March 27, 1964, the strongest earthquake to ever occur in North America happened in **southern Alaska**, about 75 miles (121 km) east of Anchorage, Alaska. It was a 9.2 magnitude earthquake. It shook the ground in downtown Anchorage for a full five minutes. The earthquake killed nine people. It created a massive tsunami, the most destructive to ever strike the west coast of the United States and Canada. It killed 106 people in Alaska, 4 in Oregon, and 11 in Crescent City, California. The wave was at a height of 220 feet (67 m) when it struck the Valdez Inlet in Alaska and had declined to 21 feet (6.4 m) by the time it hit California. The tsunami moved along the coast at a speed of 500 miles per hour (805 km/hr).

Aftermath of Alaska 1964 tsunami.
Photo credit: NOAA

On July 17, 1998, an underwater earthquake in the southwestern Pacific near **Papua New Guiana** caused a tsunami. Approximately 2, 202 people were killed.

On December 26, 2004, a tsunami in the **Indian Ocean** hit the coast of South Asia, killing more than 220,000 people. The tsunami hit more than 11 countries in the region, including Thailand, Malaysia, Indonesia, Burma, Sri Lanka, India and Somalia. Waves even hit Africa, which is about 3,000 miles (4,828 km) away from the origin of the tsunami. The hardest hit area was the northwestern tip of the Indonesian island of Sumatra. The epicenter of the earthquake that caused the tsunami was only 150 miles (241 km) offshore of the island, and about 18 miles (29 km) below the surface of the ocean. Lasting almost a full nine minutes, the earthquake that caused the tsunami was the third most powerful earthquake ever measured. The earthquake that caused the Indian Ocean tsunami of 2004 measured 9.0 on the Richter scale. It was the most powerful earthquake in over 40 years. It ruptured a section of the ocean crust 750 miles (1,200 km) long and 60 miles (100 km) wide. It moved rocks approximately 50 feet (15 m) in as little as three minutes.

Chapter 7: Studying

Scientists study tsunamis to try to figure out where and how they started. This not only helps them to predict and warn people about where the current waves may travel, it also provides insights into ways to predict tsunamis in the future. They use a variety of tools to study tsunamis, including computers, seismographs, and models, such as the SWASH (Simulating Waves until at Shore) model, used to calculate how tall a wave is, how fast it's moving, and how much energy it holds.

Scientists study a variety of aspects of tsunamis in an effort to learn more about them so changes can be made that may help to save lives. They do this by compiling the data they collect to help understand and predict tsunami events and where and how they might strike. For instance, they may study the shape of the ocean floor and the coastlines and put the information into a computer so that they can predict how tall a tsunami in the area might be and what part of the coastline is vulnerable to flooding. In doing this, scientists can predict with fair accuracy which areas are likely to be the worst hit during a tsunami and steps can be taken to put practices into place that promote public safety. For example, "tsunami evacuation zones" can be created in places that are vulnerable and laws can be established that forbid building structures in the areas prone to damage from tsunamis.

Safety

If you are in an area where there is a high risk for a tsunami, some steps can be taken to help keep you safe in the event of a tsunami. Above all, be aware of how high above sea level you are, whether you live in the area or are visiting. Figure out how far away you are from the coast. Make a plan to get to higher ground in case of a tsunami warning. Make sure everyone in your family knows what the plan is. Keep emergency supplies on hand and have them in a place where you can get to them quickly. These should include a flashlight, batteries, a first-aid kit, a battery-operated radio, necessary prescription medications, blankets, and food and water.

When a *tsunami watch* has been issued, stay away from the beach. Watch and listen to the weather radio or news for more information. When a *tsunami warning* has been issued, move to higher ground immediately, taking your emergency supplies with you. Move quickly. Just a matter of moments can save lives.

Conclusion

While tsunamis carry potential for devastating destruction, many factors can reduce the damage, particularly awareness and preparation as well as education and research. Understanding how tsunamis form and develop and knowing what steps to take when one strikes can minimalize the damage that may result from these natural disasters. Advancements in early warning systems in recent years have made a critical difference in helping to save lives in the future.

Bibliography

Australian Government Bureau of Meteorology. "Tsunami Facts and Information." http://www.bom.gov.au/tsunami/info/

Fine, Jill. Tsunamis. Children's Press: New York. 2007.

Fradin, Judy and Dennis. *Tsunamis: Witness to Disaster*. National Geographic: Washington, D.C. 2008.

González, Frank I. "Tsunami!" *Scientific American, 280*, 56–65 (1999). http://www.pmel.noaa.gov/pubs/outstand/gonz2088/gonz2088.shtml

Hamilton, John. *Tsunamis*. ABDO Daughters: Edina, Minnesota. 2006

Mott, Maryann. "Did Animals Sense the Tsunami Was Coming?" *National Geographic News*, January 4, 2005. **http://news.nationalgeographic.com/news/2005/01/0104_050104_tsunami_animals.html**

NOAA brochure. "Tsunami: the Great Waves." **http://www.nws.noaa.gov/om/brochures/tsunami2.htm**

NOAA Center for Tsunami Research. "DART® (Deep-ocean Assessment and Reporting of Tsunamis." **http://nctr.pmel.noaa.gov/Dart/**

NOAA's National Weather Service, Pacific Tsunami Warning Center. "Frequently Asked Questions (FAQ)." **http://ptwc.weather.gov/faq.php**

Oregon Department of Geology and Industries website. "Geologic Hazards on the Oregon CoastThe science of tsunamis." **http://www.oregongeology.com/sub/earthquakes/coastal/Science ofTsunamis.htm**

United Nations Educational, Scientific and Cultural Organization (UNESCO): Intergovernmental Oceanographic Commission website. "Indian Ocean Tsunami Warning System performed well, detailed assessment underway." April 13, 2012. **http://www.unesco.org/new/en/natural-sciences/ioc-oceans/single-view-oceans/news/indian_ocean_wide_tsunami_watch/**

United States Geological Survey (USGS) Earthquake Hazards Program website. "The Richter Scale." **http://earthquake.usgs.gov/learn/topics/richter.php**

University of Hawaii at Hilo's Natural Hazards Big Island website. "Understanding the difference between a tsunami "watch" and "warning." **http://www.uhh.hawaii.edu/~nat_haz/tsunamis/watchvwarning.php**

The Science of Tornadoes

Introduction

You can feel when a tornado is on the way: the thunderstorm that has been raging stops abruptly and the air becomes absolutely still, as if all of the energy has been sucked right out of it. The scent of wet, damp earth hovers all around. The sky looks greenish-yellow and the unexpected quiet is disturbing. This is when you know a tornado is in the area. This is when you know it may be time to seek shelter in a safe place, like a basement or a culvert.

While some areas in the world experience few or no tornadoes, including most of Africa and all of Antarctica, most areas in the world do experience tornadoes. Outside of the United States, they occur most frequently in northern Europe, western Asia, Bangladesh, Japan, Australia, and New Zealand. The United States, however, has more strong tornadoes than anywhere else, averaging about 800 a year. They cause approximately 80 deaths in the U.S. every year and 1, 500 injuries. They occur most frequently in an area known as "Tornado Alley," a broad band that stretches across the Great Plains between the Appalachian and Rocky Mountains. The ten states that experience the most tornadoes are Texas, Oklahoma, Florida, Kansas, Nebraska, Iowa, Missouri, Illinois, South Dakota, and Louisiana, but tornadoes have been known to occur in other states, too, such as Ohio and Massachusetts.

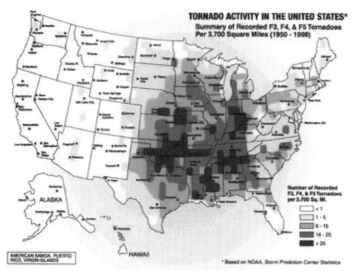

Tornado activity in the U.S.

Each state in the U.S. has its own tornado season. In the southern states, for instance, peak tornado season runs from March through May, but peak tornado season in the northern states is during the summer months. Tornadoes tend to be more common when warm afternoons and cool mornings and evenings create ideal conditions for severe thunderstorms. These severe thunderstorms can generate tornadoes when they release a high level of energy. One-quarter of all tornadoes strike between the hours of 3 PM and 9 PM. Most last less than ten minutes, but some can last hours.

Tornadoes have differing levels of power and can be categorized as "weak," "strong," and "violent." Violent tornadoes can wreak great destruction in a very brief time. They can flatten homes and barns, lift trains and semi-trucks into the air, and even pick up a car and carry it from one place to another. One lifted a hotel sign in Oklahoma and carried it 30 miles over state lines to drop it in Arkansas. The high-speed winds of a tornado can turn everyday objects – such as nails, pieces of glass, tree branches and even blades of grass – into deadly missiles. While most tornadoes are less than 1, 600 feet in diameter, some can be up to 2 miles wide. They range in speed from 35 mph to 60 mph. Some may only travel a few feet while others can plow a path of destruction 50 miles long. Winds inside a tornado may reach speeds up to 300 mph.

The U.S. has a long history of tornadoes, with some years being worse than others. More tornadoes form in some years than in other years. For instance, in April 1974, 148 tornadoes were reported within a 24-hour period, forming in groups as storms moved across the U.S. The incident came to be known as the "Super Outbreak." Altogether, 13 U.S. states were affected as well as parts of Canada. One of the tornadoes during this outbreak demolished close to 3,000 buildings in Xenia, Ohio. This was the most extensive outbreak of tornadoes in the U.S. to date.

Tornadoes also make history based on other aspects. The deadliest U.S. tornadoes, for instance, occurred on March 18, 1925. It killed 695 people as it plowed a 219-mile long track across parts of Missouri, Illinois, and Indiana. The biggest known tornado on record was reported on May 22, 2004 in Hallam, Nebraska. The tornado had a peak width of close to two and a half miles. The costliest tornado on record struck Joplin, Montana on May 22, 2011 and caused an estimated $2.8 billion in damage.

Tornadoes inspire a mix of emotions in people: awe, fear, wonder, terror. This is due to quickness with which a tornado develops and its potential for complete devastation. A tornado can sometimes form in a minute or less. It can beat sound brick houses into piles of rubble in an instant. It can travel across the ground at high speeds, and then suddenly vanish. It can kill in a matter of seconds. What's behind these incredible forces of nature? Where do they come from and how do they form?

Chapter 1: What Is a Tornado?

A tornado, by definition, is a violently spinning column of air in contact with the ground. The column must touch the ground and it must extend from the ground to the base of a cloud to officially be named a tornado. A tornado is pendant (meaning that is hangs downward) from a cumuliform cloud or underneath a cumuliform cloud (a cumuliform cloud is a type of cloud that develops vertically, forming rising mounds, domes, or towers). It actually consists of nothing more than air and water vapor. The air in the tornado's column is whirling, or moving horizontally, and also rising, or moving vertically. The water vapor is condensing and creating heat and energy.

Tornadoes form during violent thunderstorms, but they do not form with every violent thunderstorm. They form in what are known as a "supercell," which is a thunderstorm with a deep rotating updraft. Only about one in a thousand thunderstorms produces a tornado. The conditions in the thunderstorm have to be just right. Tornadoes develop when the air is unstable and warm, moist air masses meet cold, dry air masses.

A tornado is a fairly organized structure. It consists of a vortex – a whirling mass of air – that moves at very high speeds with the air of the mass rising in an upward spiral. The air enters the vortex at its base, near the ground and exits at the top, near the clouds. The air rushes inward toward a low pressure in the center and rises upward within the outer wall of the tornado. Debris that is caught up in the mass of rising air can be lifted and carried several miles above the surface of the earth. The vortex can extend several miles above the ground.

The whirling air and the rising air of the vortex often move at the same speed, but this can vary. For instance, the whirling air may be moving at a speed of 70 miles per hour and the rising air may also be moving at a speed at 70 miles per hour, or the whirling air may be moving at 70 miles per hour and the rising air at 100 miles per hour. If the speed of the upward air greatly exceeds the speed of the whirling air, it creates an internal vacuum that will then suck up anything the tornado passes over. It is then capable of lifting heavy objects and doing extensive damage. When the tornado touches a building, its fierce winds have the ability to tear the building apart.

A tornado will move across the earth at varying speeds. Most move at a speed of approximately 30 mph, but they may speed up or slow down or even stand still at any point. They can abruptly change direction and have been known to do U-turns or figure-8s. Mountains will sometimes stop a tornado, but some have been reported to move over mountains. Once a tornado is in motion, it will continue to move until it dissipates, which occurs when its air circulations are interrupted due to cool, stable low-level air flowing into the tornado.

Not all whirling air masses can be defined as a tornado. For instance, a cyclone, which has many properties that are similar the tornadoes – including containing as vortex with wind speeds that can reach up to 500 mph – is formed differently than a tornado. It forms when an area of low pressure moves over water. Likewise "dust devils" are similar to tornadoes in that they are a vertically oriented rotating column of air, but, unlike tornadoes, they arise as a swirling updraft of air. Neither cyclones nor dust devils are formed by parent clouds, which is a key factor in the formation of tornadoes. Most tornadoes are created in supercell thunderstorms, which makes them a distinctive weather phenomenon.

Chapter 2: What Does a Tornado Look Like?

When you see a tornado, it will appear to be hanging down from a storm cloud and will extend to the ground. Signs of debris below the funnel identify it as a tornado. Its tip – the part that touches the ground – will move over the earth, often whipping back and forth like a tail. While most tornadoes will have the classic funnel-shape, they can appear in other forms as well. Some are long and narrow like ropes and others are stocky, like a barrel. The classic image of a funnel-shaped tornado which is wide at the top and narrow at the bottom is its most common form. The form a tornado takes and how it looks depends on several factors, including air pressure, temperature, moisture, dust, the rate the air is moving into the tornado and whether the air at its core is rising or falling. Often what we see when we look at a tornado is the bottom 10 percent of the vortex protruding from the base of a thunderstorm – the rest of the vortex is inside the thunderstorm.

It is not always easy to see a tornado. Some tornadoes are clearly visible while others may be obscured by rain or nearby low-hanging clouds. They vary in color, depending on the material they pick up as well as the amount and direction of light and the level of humidity in the air. They have been described as being black, red, gray, orange, or purple. Tornadoes will appear almost transparent until they pick up dust and debris. A tornado crossing over an area of red clay, for instance, might take on a reddish hue, while a tornado picking up rich topsoil over farmland may appear almost black. A tornado traveling over a snow-covered area may turn white. The color of a tornado is also influenced by the surrounding cloud cover and the direction from which the tornado is viewed in respect to the sun. A tornado that forms in an area with lots of humid air surrounding it may appear black, gray, or white depending on which way the light hits it. A tornado may even appear pink if the angle of the sun is low.

A white tornado

Many metaphors – figures of speech used to describe how something looks – have been used to describe how a tornado appears. Metaphors observers of tornadoes commonly use compare the appearance of a tornado to a snake, a writhing rope, or the moving trunk of an elephant. Some people have described them as looking like a giant barrel or the stem of a mushroom, and like an hourglass or the Liberty Bell.

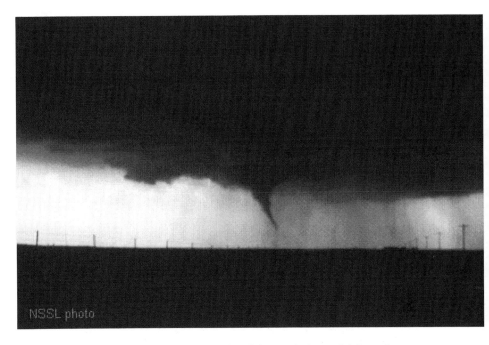

This photo was taken within a few seconds of the one below, and from the opposite direction (along the same roadway). Here, much of the sunlight is absorbed by tens of thousands of feet of thunderstorm cloud material, leaving the tornado "backlit," or silhouetted, by the light to the west. The following image shows the same tornado from the opposite direction. "Photo courtesy of NSSL"

This is the same tornado as in the previous picture, at almost the same instant, from about the same distance, in nearly the opposite direction. It appears front-lit by filtered (refracted) sunlight streaming in from the west (behind the photographer). Fuzzy gray areas beneath the cloud base at right are precipitation curtains wrapping southward around the west edge of the mesocyclone. "Photo courtesy of NSSL"

Although most tornadoes form as a single vortex, some storms will produce a large tornado that has several smaller tornadoes within it. This is called a "multi-vortex" tornado. It is much larger and wider than a single tornado and can do much more damage. It is recognizable by its multiple funnels. Multi-vortex tornados have been described as looking like bands of ribbons whirling in the sky or like eggbeaters.

Chapter 3: How Does a Tornado Start?

The simple answer regarding the question of how a tornado starts is that cold, dry air moving from one direction meets warm, moist air moving from another direction. The cold air is heavier and pushes beneath the warm air, causing the warm air to swiftly rise. When this happens, a thunderstorm is created and the air begins to rotate or spin. Although there are many other ingredients that cause a tornado to start, scientists do not yet fully understand them. One aspect that is consistent is that areas where warm air and cool air clash create conditions that are ideal for the start of a tornado.

You can see how this all plays out in the area known as Tornado Alley. The weather conditions in this region are just right for the formation of tornadoes for a number of reasons. First, the tropical, humid air that tends to hang above the Gulf of Mexico is blown north by wind. Second, cold, dry air blows south from Canada. Third, hot dry air from the southwest desert region creates a "dry line" – a border – between itself and the humid Gulf air. For a while, the dry line keeps the humid Gulf air from rising. Eventually, however, the moist Gulf air breaks through the dry line, which is weakened from the constant pressure between the hot, dry air and the warm, moist air. When this happens, the moist Gulf air shoots upward at a great speed and can create a "supercell" thunderstorm – a type of thunderstorm that has prime conditions for producing tornadoes – within minutes. The jetstream (the current of air that runs from west to east across the U.S.) then fuels the mix, churning the warm and cool air masses. This creates the potential for the formation of tornadoes.

What is a supercell thunderstorm and why is it prime breeding ground for a tornado? A supercell thunderstorm is a storm with a deep and concentrated rotating updraft. The rotating area is known as a "mesocyclone." Sometimes, the mesocyclone in a supercell will form into a tornado. The exact process behind this formation is not yet fully understood by scientists. Part of the mystery is that scientists do not yet understand exactly what causes the rotation and how it becomes so concentrated. We will examine the supercell relationship to tornado formation in greater detail in a later section.

While supercell thunderstorms produce the most powerful, violent, and destructive tornadoes, weaker tornadoes may form along a squall line (a narrow band of high winds and storms associated with a cold front), on the fringes of supercells, and under growing cumulus clouds. While supercell tornadoes take many hours to form, these weaker tornadoes form and disperse quickly. They may still do considerable damage due to strong winds, but they are not as intense and do not last as long. They do not develop mesocyclones, with the exception of some squall line tornados. These may develop a mesocyclone, but the entire structure of the storm does not rotate, as it does in a supercell tornado. As with supercell tornadoes, these weaker varieties of tornadoes start when a cold air mass clashes with a warm air mass.

Chapter 4: What Does a Tornado Sound Like?

The sound a tornado makes has been described in many ways. Some people say it makes a "rumbling" sound, while others say it sounds like a "whoosh." Others say it sounds like a "whine" or a "roar." A "hissing" or "swishing" sound has sometimes been observed. It has been described as being like the whine of the engine of a jet airplane during takeoff, or like the sound of the wind blowing through open car windows. A tornado may make a loud and steady whooshing noise, like a waterfall.

Tornadoes emit sound for a number of reasons. Some researchers hypothesize that the sounds may be caused by the circulation of air masses within the tornado. These eddying masses create vibrations and generate sounds. How much sound is put out is dependent on the intensity of the tornado. Wind speeds of a higher velocity (or speed) will produce stronger vibrations than lower velocity winds, and will thus make more sound.

Exactly what sort of noise a tornado makes depends on many things. The National Weather Service Storm Prediction Center cites many factors that may influence the sound of a tornado, including proximity, or how close or far a tornado is when you hear it. If a tornado is in the distance, for instance, the sound is often compared to being like a passing freight train – like a rumble in the distance. Unlike a freight train, however, the rumble remains steady and does not pass. When a tornado is nearby, however, the sound increases in volume, building to a "roar" that is said to be "deafening." This is due not only to the noise caused by the high-speed of the winds in the tornado, but also to the noise of the damage it causes as it travels. The position of the tornado at the time you hear it will also influence how it sounds. A tornado that is directly overhead, for instance, may sound like "the buzzing of a huge swarm of bees," which is a phrase frequently used to describe the sound that comes from the center of a tornado.

Intensity (the speed of the tornadoes winds) and size (its width) are other factors that may figure into how a tornado sounds. Researchers have noted, for instance, that you have to be within a mile of an F2 tornado to hear it, while a more intense and stronger tornado, such as a F4, may be heard as far away as 4 miles. Regardless, neither of these is a great amount of distance when it comes to tornadoes, and so if you can hear a tornado, you should take shelter immediately.

Chapter 5: What Are the Warnings That a Tornado Is Coming?

One of the first visible warning signs that a tornado is forming is dust swirling upward toward a funnel cloud hanging from the base of a parent cloud. In the early stages, the dust and the cloud will not appear connected. The presence of one without the other is not an indication of a tornado. A funnel cloud can form at the base of a parent cloud, for instance, but it is not considered a tornado. Swirling dust on its own may merely be a dust devil – a swirling updraft of air non-related to a thunderstorm.

Other obvious warning signs that a tornado is in the area include:

- the sky turns dark and yellowish-green
- very large hail
- a sudden dead calm or fast shift in the wind after rain or hail have been falling
- a loud roar or rumbling sound similar to the sound of a freight train that doesn't fade
- the underside of a thunderstorm cloud spins swiftly
- dust or debris under a thunderstorm cloud is whirling
- power lines snap

While visible warning signs are helpful for knowing when a tornado may be forming in the area, scientists have devised elaborate methods over the years that can track and forecast tornadoes. These include weather satellites and weather balloons.

Launching a weather balloon.

While the satellites and balloons are not capable of actually spotting tornadoes, they can identify supercells and other thunderstorms and track the movements of these storms by gathering information about temperature, pressure, wind speed, and direction. Using this data, forecasters can then use computers to help predict where thunderstorms capable of generating tornadoes might form over the next 12 to 24 hours.

Scientists also use a radar system called "Doppler" to measure wind speeds and other atmospheric phenomenon that may indicate the presence of tornadoes in an area. Created by Austrian physicist Christian Doppler, the radar system is capable of detecting and measuring motion. It works by sending out radio waves via an antenna. When the waves hit evidence of weather activity in the atmosphere, such as raindrops or hail, the radio waves bounce back to the antenna. The patterns of the radio waves are used to generate an image that shows where the activity is occurring. It can also show the direction and speed of wind using changes in the frequency of the waves. For instance, as rain moves away from the antenna, the pattern stretches out. As it moves toward it, the pattern condenses. Doppler was installed in U.S. weather stations in the 1980s and 1990s. A clear sign that a tornado may be developing is when an image known as a "hook echo" appears on the radar screen. The image is shaped like a fishhook and indicates a storm has a rotating motion that may spawn tornadoes.

Mobile radar.

Volunteer storm spotters are also used to help forecast tornadoes. They are individuals who have been trained to observe the skies and recognize the warning signs of developing tornadoes, such as signs of severe storms gathering or the rotation of winds that may signal the beginning of funnel clouds. The volunteers are engaged nationwide to report suspicious weather activity to the National Weather Service. During weather alerts, the volunteers are strategically stationed by a coordinator to confirm findings reported by Doppler and computers.

Once a tornado sighting is reported in an area, a tornado warning is issued by the National Weather Service. A "warning" differs from a "watch" in that it means an actual tornado has been spotted. A "watch" indicates that the weather conditions for tornado formation are present in an area.

Chapter 6: Life Cycle of a Tornado

Supercell Relation

As noted, a supercell is a thunderstorm with a deep and concentrated rotating updraft known as a mesocyclone. Supercells need four main components to develop: wind shear, moisture, instability, and lift.

Wind shear is created when wind at one height moves in a different direction or speed than wind at another height. This creates a spinning tube of air. Once wind shear is present, it can cause warm air to lift rapidly and meet cold air that is higher up. As the rapidly rising warmer air lifts into higher cold air, it creates an unstable air mass. This can produce the conditions necessary for a thunderstorm to form. As the warm air rises and forms moisture as it cools in the colder air, the moisture develops into clouds that can generate very heavy rains and hail.

The final element required to form a supercell is a source of lift. Lift is a mechanism that starts an updraft in the moist, unstable airmass. One source of lift may be differential heating, which occurs when one area heats faster than another area. This may be a result of portions of the earth's surface being heated more readily by the sun than other portions. Another source of lift may be advancing cold fronts or warm fronts, such as what is seen when the air from the Gulf of Mexico meets with the air blowing in from Canada.

As the warm air continues to rise and produces more moisture, the heat and energy may provide enough fuel to eventually form the intensely rotating thunderstorm known as a supercell. A supercell can be quite powerful. The rotating area within a supercell, the mesocyclone, is positioned as a vertical column between the wall and the top of the supercell. The mesocyclone can form into a tornado if the right conditions are present, although scientists do not fully understand why this happens. As long as the mesocyclone is inside the thunderstorm cloud, however, it is not a tornado. It has to touch to ground to become a tornado. Less than 20 percent of supercells actually generate tornadoes.

Formation

The mesocyclone may eventually cause a cloud to drop down below it as it spins. This cloud is called a "wall cloud." It is free of rain and it rotates. It is in this cloud that tornadoes can form, although scientists are not yet sure how this occurs. They haven't discovered the mechanism that causes a tornado to appear between the wall cloud and the ground. They suspect it may be caused by the rear flank downdraft (RFD) – a powerful downward burst of air near the back of the supercell. The RFD plunges downward and spreads out, creating a gust front. This gust front of the RFD may sweep around the existing spinning air of the mesocyclone, distorting it and dragging it downward. If the RFD wraps around the spinning air between the wall cloud and the ground and squeezes it in the right way as it forces it to the ground, the spinning air may become a tornado. Scientists further theorize that the RFD has to connect back into the supercell to produce the tornado. While the RFD theory make sense, more data needs to be gathered before scientists can fully solve the mystery of how tornados form between the wall cloud and the ground.

Once the conditions that form tornadoes are present, more than one tornado can form. A group of tornados may be formed by a single thunderstorm and will share a similar path. Such a group is called a "family" of tornadoes. Occasionally, a single tornado may develop more than one funnel. Such tornadoes are called "multiple vortex" tornadoes. When dozens of tornadoes form from multiple thunderstorms over an area, it is called a "tornado outbreak."

Maturity

A tornado is considered "mature" when it is vertical and touching the ground. Once the tornado touches the ground, an ample flow of warm, moist air continues to flow into via an updraft. This fuels the tornado and causes it to grow in power. At this point, the tornado is capable of causing destruction to anything in its path. It is at its greatest size and strength. Depending on the interplay of the warm, moist updrafts and the RFD within it, a mature tornado can last less than 8 minutes or maintain an intense and deadly power for well over an hour.

Dissipation

As the RFD continues to wrap around the tornado, it gradually cuts off the inflow of warm, moist air and the tornado begins to shrink and lessen in intensity. Even as it weakens, however, it is still capable of causing damage. It may even actually speed up as its size decreases. As the inflow of warm, moist air continues to decrease, the tornado's funnel tilts. The lower end of the tornado lags behind the upper part. Eventually the wall cloud disappears. Once the inflow into the funnel stops completely, the tornado becomes narrow and rope-like in appearance as it is moved about by upward and downward spirals of air. The "rope" can stretch out for a mile or more. This stage can last as long as ten minutes or more. Eventually the tornado dissipates into a diffuse mass of air.

Early stage of tornado formation.

The tornado continues developing.

Tornado in a mature state of development.

Tornado in its dying stage. "Photo courtesy of NSSL"

Chapter 7: Different Kinds of Tornadoes

Supercell Tornadoes

Tornadoes that originate in supercell thunderstorms are the most powerful of tornadoes. They are distinguished from weaker tornadoes by the presence of a mesocyclone, their long formation period, and their capacity to become very powerful. Supercell tornadoes are able to retain their structure for several hours, although many last for only brief periods of time. These tornadoes take on a variety of shapes:

- *Wedge Tornado.* A wedge tornado looks wider than its distance from the ground to the base of the cloud. Many factors, including size, moisture content, and cloud height, can affect the width of a tornado. Many observers cannot tell the difference between a low-hanging cloud and a wedge tornado from a distance. Even though they are wider than other kinds of tornadoes, wedge tornadoes are not necessarily stronger. Because of their extreme width, however, they have a wide damage path.

A wedge tornado.

- *Stovepipe Tornado.* A stovepipe tornado is cylindrical in shape. It appears thick and even from top to bottom, like a tree trunk.
- *Rain-wrap Tornado.* A rain-wrap tornado is surrounded by rain and can be dangerously hidden by it.
- *Rope Tornado.* While most tornados assume the shape of a rope in their final moments as they die out, a rope tornado holds this shape throughout its life cycle. It is long and thin like a piece of rope but can be very powerful despite being so narrow.

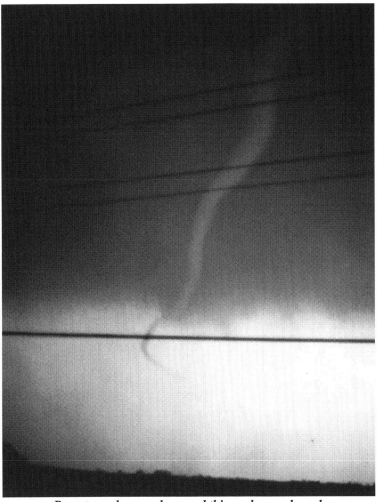

Rope tornadoes are long and thin and rope-shaped.

- *Elephant Trunk Tornado.* An elephant trunk tornado tapers to a narrow point and looks like the trunk of an elephant. Its bottom moves from side to side along the ground, like an elephant searching for food with its trunk.
- *Multi-vortex Tornado.* A multi-vortex tornado contains two or more small, intense subvortexes that orbit within the center of the larger tornado vortex. They can occur in all kinds of tornado shapes. The subvortexes can form and die within a matter of seconds.

Landspout

Landspouts form on the fringes of supercell thunderstorms or beneath cumulus clouds. They form when two air masses meet. As the two air masses slide past each other, the air begins to swirl in eddies along the boundaries. When a cumulus cloud moves over the swirling air, an updraft is created and the swirl is pulled upward. Landspouts form from the ground up, as opposed to tornadoes that originate in supercell storms. They are technically considered tornadoes since they consist of an intensely rotating column of air in contact with both the surface of the earth and a cumuliform cloud. While they are generally weaker and smaller than supercell tornadoes, they are capable of doing considerable damage due to their strong winds.

Waterspout

Waterpouts are an intensely rotating column of air that forms over the ocean or over a lake. Waterspouts can be either tornadic or non-tornadic. Non-tornadic waterspouts are not associated with supercell thunderstorms and are the more common type. They are short-lived and may develop and dissipate within 20 minutes. Like their counterparts on land – landspouts – they frequently form under cumulus clouds. Non-tornadic waterspouts tend to move slowly, with winds of less than 30 mph. They are not very powerful. Tornadic waterspouts, on the other hand, can be quite powerful. They develop in a manner similar to supercell tornadoes. Tornadic waterspouts form in connection with severe thunderstorms and develop a mesocyclone. They are not very common in the U. S.

Other Tornado-like Weather Phenomenon

While the following are not technically tornadoes, they are similar in some ways and are often considered to be "cousins" of true tornadoes.

Gustnado

A gustnado is smaller and weaker than a tornado, but strong enough to do minor damage to a car or the roof of a house. Gustnados are short-lived – often lasting only a few seconds or minutes. A gustnado is not generated by a supercell and is not connected to a cloud base. Instead, it forms along the gusty and windy front of a thunderstorm or squall line as fast moving cold, dry air is blown through a mass of stationary, warm, moist air.

Dust Devil

A dust devil is a column of whirling air that forms under clear skies. Its formation is not associated with clouds in any way. Dust devils may develop when a strong draft of convective air forms near the ground during very hot temperatures. If there is enough wind shear present, a dust devil may build up a cyclonic action.

A dust devil.

Fire Whirls
Fire whirls are vertical tornado-like swirls of air that form near very hot air or fires, such as near wildfires. They are generally not connected to clouds. Though they are not strong, they can produce considerable damage, mainly due to uprooting trees and helping wildfires to spread.

Chapter 8: Classifying Tornadoes

Meteorologists use the Fujita Scale to measure the strength of tornadoes. The original Fujita Scale, which measured tornadoes on a scale of F0 to F5, with F5 being the most destructive, was devised in 1971 by tornado expert Tetsuya "Ted" Fujita of the University of Chicago in collaboration with Allen Pearson, head of the National Severe Storms Forecast Center. On that scale, an F0 rated tornado, the least destructive, had wind speeds of 40-72 mph and an F5 rated tornado, the most destructive, had wind speeds of over 261 mph. But scientists came to realize that this scale often over-rated wind speeds for stronger tornadoes, meaning they saw the wind speeds that could create extreme damage were actually less than what they had rated them. So in 2007, meteorologists introduced the Enhanced Fujita Scale (EF) as a way to categorize tornadoes. It divides tornadoes into six categories from EF0 to EF5, also based on the strength and wind speeds of tornadoes. In the new and revised rating system, however, an EF0 tornado has an estimated wind speed of 65-85 mph and is capable of light damage to roofs and tree limbs while an EF5 tornado has an estimated wind speed of more than 200 mph (as opposed to 261 mph on the old scale) and is capable of total destruction, such as the leveling of entire neighborhoods and towns. The EF system is more accurate in rating the wind speeds of stronger tornadoes that the original Fujita Scale and is able to better estimate the potential damage a tornado can cause. The EF system also includes up 28 "damage indicators," which are specific ways to measure the damage done by a tornado. Some examples of damage indicators in the EF system are "small retail building (fast food)," "automobile showroom," and "tree – hardwood." The damage done to any of these damage indicators provides information that allows wind speed to be guessed with fairly accurately.

You may wonder *how* scientists are able to actually measure the wind speed of a tornado in order to categorize them. The conventional method is to measure the wind speed at the center of a tornado using an instrument known as an "anemometer." These instruments are available in many designs, with the most common consisting of small cups mounted at the end of horizontal arms. The arms can turn freely and spin when the wind blows. The rate they spin at is converted into wind speed. Other designs measure the pressure of the wind and convert it into wind speed. A drawback of anemometers is that the devices may blow apart and be destroyed in severely high winds.

Doppler radar can also be used to measure the wind speed of tornadoes. This is achieved by sending a beam of microwaves from the dish of the radar toward the tornado. Wind speed measurements are based on the pattern of the waves as they deflect off of the debris and raindrops or hail in the wind. The strongest wind speed measured in a tornado by a mobile Doppler radar, according to the National Severe Storms Laboratory website, was 318 mph on May 3, 1999 near Bridge Creek/Moore, Oklahoma.

Chapter 9: Notable Tornadoes in Recent Years

While tornadoes are generally rare phenomenon, they do occur. When they do strike, they often do mild or very little damage. Some tornadoes, however, can be violent, severe, and extremely destructive. They can kill a great number of people and level entire towns. Unfortunately, these are the tornadoes people most people remember. These are the storms that often come to mind whenever a tornado warning is sounded. Not all tornadoes are like these, but a handful of tornado incidents in recent times provide evidence of the potential for devastation tornadoes are capable of rendering.

The Super Outbreak

On April 3rd and April 4th of 1974, one of the largest outbreaks of tornadoes ever to hit the United States struck, beginning in Tennessee and Georgia at 2 p.m. and spreading over 13 Midwestern and southern states throughout the night and into the morning, lasting a total of 16 hours. By the time the storms had stopped, 148 tornadoes had been reported. 368 people were killed and 5,484 had been injured during the storms. The tornadoes ranged in size from F0 to F5. An F5 tornado struck the town of Xenia, Ohio, leveling over 1,000 homes and killing 34 people. Although it was considered the worst outbreak ever to hit the U.S. at the time, the number of tornados in the April 2011 tornado surpasses the Super Outbreak.

Oklahoma City Outbreak

On May 3, 1999, an outbreak of 74 tornadoes ranging in size from F0 to F5 hit Central Oklahoma. At one point, four tornadoes were reported to all be on the ground at the same time. What makes this outbreak most notable, though, is the F5 tornado that hit the suburbs of Oklahoma City, lasting for more than an hour and traveling 38 miles in that time. The tornado's base was reported to be more than a quarter of a mile wide. More than 8,000 homes were damaged or destroyed. Luckily, the loss of lives and injuries was comparatively low despite the tornado's deadly potential, due to advance warning. The storms had been tracked with radar and helicopters and forecasters were able to give people fifteen or more minutes of warning before the F5 tornado struck. When the storms were over, only 46 people were dead and 800 injured.

Hallam, Nebraska Tornado

With a width of more almost two and a half miles, the tornado that struck Hallam, Nebraska on May 22, 2004 is currently the largest reported tornado on record. It received a rating of F4 after lifting homes off of their foundations and tossing several cars and a school bus. The tornado was part of an outbreak of 56 tornadoes that struck several midwestern states that evening, with most of the tornadoes touching down in Iowa and Nebraska. Only one fatality and 38 injuries were reported. The hook echo – one of the classic features of a tornado-producing supercell thunderstorm when viewed on radar – completely engulfed the town of Hallam on the radar when the tornado was at its widest.

The Greensburg Tornado

Despite the severity of the tornado that struck the town of
Greensburg, Kansas on May 4, 2007, only 12 people died and only
60 were injured. This was due in large part to the ample warning
given to the town's residents, who heard the sirens going off for a
full twenty minutes before the tornado's arrival. The tornado was
rated EF5 and destroyed 95 percent of the buildings in the town. It
was so large and contained so much debris that it could actually be
viewed on the radar image. The tornado's path was almost 2 miles
wide – as wide as the town. Even though it caused massive
destruction to the buildings and property of Greensburg, the
advanced warning gave people enough time to seek shelter, therefore
saving hundreds of lives.

April 2011 Tornado Outbreaks

The month of April in 2011 was a record month for tornadoes. The
National Oceanic and Atmospheric Administration's website lists
758 tornadoes reported during the entire month, with most of them
reported during two of the worst tornado outbreaks in the history of
the U.S. The first outbreak occurred on April 14-16 and was
followed two weeks later by the second outbreak on April 25-28.
The April 14-16 outbreak resulted in at least 200 tornadoes reported
in 16 states. A total of 38 people were killed. The three-day outbreak
began in the Great Plains on the first day, moved into Mississippi
and Alabama on the second, and then progressed through the
Carolinas and Virginia on the third day. During the April 25-28
outbreak, 305 tornadoes were reported in 21 states. The outbreak
resulted in 321 deaths, making it one of the deadliest two-day
periods for tornado in history.

There are several theories regarding why the month of April 2011 saw so many tornadoes. Some scientists speculate that global warming and carbon emissions may be a factor, but there is currently no conclusive evidence that this is true. Another factor cited is higher than usual water temperatures in the Gulf of Mexico that year, which provided plenty of warm, moist air as "fuel" for severe storm systems. A third factor may be the presence of the strongest El Nina patterns in recorded history present during 2011. The El Nina pattern caused great contrasts in air masses, with cool and dry air to the north and warm and steamy air to the south, over the Mississippi Valley at that time.

Joplin, Montana Tornado

One of the costliest tornados to strike in recent times was the EF5 tornado that struck Joplin, Montana on May 22, 2011. The tornado caused an estimated $2.8 billion in damage. The tornado was reported to have multiple-vortexes, a diameter more than a mile wide, and wind speeds of over 200 mph. The tornado lasted approximately 45 minutes and traveled just a little over 22 miles. It took the National Weather Service damage team two days to fully assess the damage of the storm and grade it as an EF5. They did so by taking into consideration such indicators as the "shear destruction of well-built homes" and "buses, tractor trailers, and vans" that had been tossed "over 200 yards to several blocks." The surveyors noted that trees had been stripped of their bark and the asphalt of the Wal-Mart parking lot had been ripped up. It was also one of the deadliest tornadoes in the United States, ranked at 27 with 158 dead and more than 1,000 injured.

Conclusion

While researchers have come to understand a lot about tornadoes over the years, there is still much to learn. Data must to be collected to help scientists understand the mechanics behind the formation of these powerful and destructive storms, and the only way to do that is to study tornadoes as they occur.

Studying Tornadoes

Tornadoes are difficult to study because, unlike with other weather phenomenon such as floods, volcanic eruptions, and earthquakes, tornadoes leave nothing behind to study once they dissipate. With an earthquake, for instance, researchers can study the faults. But once a tornado is gone, it leaves nothing behind but the damage it has done. Because of this, researchers have to rely on methods other than direct observation to study tornadoes. These include documenting the damage done by looking at the area from above using photographs taken from planes and satellites and surveying the damage on the ground. These methods are expensive and time-consuming, however, and rescue work and cleanup often take priority.

Still, much can be learned by studying tornadoes, particularly when it comes to forecasting. By studying tornadoes, scientists will be able to better predict where and where tornadoes may strike. This can help to reduce the damage caused by tornadoes by giving people ample warning so that they can take the necessary precautions. Not only can it reduce damage, it can save lives. Before the National Weather Service began studying and predicting tornadoes, tornadoes killed an average of 230 people per year. Currently, that number has been cut by almost a third. Knowing when and where a tornado may strike helps people to prepare.

The scientists who study tornadoes are called "meteorologists." Centers where meteorologists research and study tornadoes include the National Severe Storms Laboratory (NSSL), NOAA's National Weather Service, the University of Oklahoma, the Tornado Project, Tornado History Project, and other organizations worldwide. In addition, most major universities have an atmospheric science program that publishes tornado-related studies.

These organizations use a variety of methods to research tornadoes, including Doppler radar, research and testing, and running numerous field programs that study tornadoes. One example of such a program is "Vortex2: A Field Experiment to Study Tornadoes from All Angles." Sponsored by the National Severe Storms Laboratory in 2009-2010 in conjunction with The National Oceanic and Atmospheric Administration (NOAA) and the National Science Foundation (NSF), the program joined more than 100 scientists, students, and staff from all over the world to collect data about tornadoes. They used a fleet of 10 mobile radars and 70 other high-tech instruments to accomplish the results. Programs such as this help scientists to better understand tornadoes and to be able to predict them with greater accuracy.

Storm Chasers

While some people chase tornadoes for the thrill of it, teams of scientists do so in order to gather data that may help them to understand more about tornadoes. Their goal in chasing a tornado is to get close enough to the tornado to track its direction and measure its wind speed. Mobile radar trucks, known as "Doppler on Wheels" (DOW), allow scientists to track tornadoes on the ground easily. Invented by storm chaser Josh Wurman, DOWs are custom built trucks that carry a Doppler antenna as well as radios and computers. It also has a satellite dish that allows the transmission of Internet data and radio and television signals. Using these vehicles, storm chasers are able to get extremely close to a tornado so that they can gather information.

Storm chasing can be very dangerous. Being out in a storm means being exposed to hail, lightning, flood-conditions, and high winds. While storm chasers are knowledgeable regarding the patterns and behavior of the tornadoes they are chasing, the tornadoes can – and sometimes will – do an abrupt 180 degree turn (a "U-turn") and head directly toward the storm chasers. Driving is one of the greatest hazards of storm-chasing. Imagine being in a car and not being able to see through the windshield at all because of heavy rain! Road conditions often become hazardous during the severe storms that produce tornadoes, as well. This can especially present a danger if a tornado does a U-turn and the wheels of the storm chasers' vehicles become stuck in deep mud so that the car cannot turn around and flee.

Still, despite the danger, useful information is often gathered. During the Vortex2 project research teams made science history by collecting data on a tornadic supercell in Goshen County, Wyoming from 20 minutes before it formed until after it dissipated. This intense examination of the tornado supplied researchers with evidence that a "secondary surge" (a second wave of air rushing down from above on a downdraft) may have sparked the genesis of the tornado. This sort of data can help meteorologists understand how tornadoes develop.

Tornado Safety

The chances that a tornado will strike a building that you are in are very small. Tornadoes are, in general, a rare event and only a small percentage of tornadoes damage buildings each year. Still, you can greatly reduce the chance of injury by knowing what to do should a tornado occur.

First, learn and understand what the various weather alerts regarding tornadoes means. A "Tornado Watch" is issued when tornadoes are possible in the area. It doesn't mean that one has been spotted, but that the weather conditions are right for them to form. When a tornado watch has been issued, you should stay alert: listen to the TV or radio for updates and know where you are going to take shelter if you must do so.

A "Tornado Warning" is issued when an observer has actually sighted a tornado or indicated by weather radar. When a tornado warning has been issued, you should take shelter immediately. If a large and violent tornado is expected to hit an area with a large population, a "Tornado Emergency" will be issued. Again, you should seek shelter in the safest spot possible at this time.

When a tornado warning or a tornado emergency has been issued, it is important to act quickly. If you are in a building or a house, you should take cover immediately in a basement or storm cellar. If that is not possible, then you should hide in a bathroom or closet on the lowest floor and protect your head with something thick, such as a mattress, metal trashcan, or bicycle helmet. Hide under something sturdy, like a workbench or staircase. A bathtub is a safe place to take shelter. Avoid windows.

If you are in a car, pull over and get out of it. One of the most dangerous places to be during a tornado is in a car or other vehicle, including mobile homes, campers, and vans. Move as far away from the vehicle as possible after you get out of it. If there is not a building to go into nearby, find a gully or ditch to lie in and cover your head. Don't hide under a bridge or highway overpass.

If you're outdoors, it is best to lie face down in a ditch or crawl into a culvert. Again, avoid cars and do not seek shelter under highway overpasses.

The best time to figure out what to do if a tornado should strike is before it strikes. Take time to make a safety plan and practice it. Your safety plan should include putting together a storm survival kit that is readily available. It should include flashlights and batteries, a battery-powered radio, bottles of water, blankets, and a first aid kit. You should also plan where to go in case a tornado strikes. Decide where the safest area in your house is – the basement, a downstairs bathroom, a neighbor's basement – and agree to gather there if a tornado should hit. Decide what you need to gather if a tornado warning is issued (such as pets and prescription medications). Once you have a plan established, practice it! Pretend a tornado warning has been issued and go through the steps of the plan. This will help you to know exactly what to do in the rare event of a tornado.

Tornadoes carry great potential for devastating destruction. They can form in no time and strike suddenly. Through a combination of education, research, awareness, and preparation, however, the damage the storms wreak can be minimalized. Understanding the mechanics of how they form and develop, knowing when and where they might strike, and being advised of what steps to take when a tornado strikes in all go a long way toward damage control. While it may be impossible to stop tornadoes from forming, information and awareness can help to save lives.

Source List

"2011 Tornado Information." National Oceanic and Atmopspheric Administration (NOAA). **http://www.noaanews.noaa.gov/2011_tornado_information.html**

"2011 Spring Tornado Outbreaks." National Severe Storms Laboratory (NSSL). **http://www.nssl.noaa.gov/news/2011/**

Allaby, Michael. Tornadoes. New York: Facts on File, Inc., 1997.

"April was record-setting month for tornadoes." *USAToday*, August 4, 2011. **http://www.usatoday.com/weather/storms/tornadoes/2011-08-04-april-tornado-record_n.htm**

Carson, Mary Kay. *Inside Tornadoes.* New York: Sterling, 2010.

Edwards, Roger. "The Online Torndao FAQ." NOAA: Storm Prediction Center. **http://www.spc.ncep.noaa.gov/faq/tornado/index.html**

Ezard, John. "Blown away." The Guardian, May 5, 1999. **http://www.guardian.co.uk/theguardian/1999/may/06/features11.g22**

Frankel, Leora. "A Storm Chaser Who's Looked Straight Into a Tornado's Heart." *Discover Magazine*, April 10, 2012. **http://discovermagazine.com/2012/extreme-earth/19-storm-chaser-looks-tornados-heart/article_view?b_start:int=1&-C**

Grazulis, Thomas P. *Tornado: Nature's Ultimate Windstorm.* Norman: University of Oklahoma Press, 2001.

Hoadley, David. "Tornado Sound Experiences." *Storm Track*, March 31, 1983. http://www.stormtrack.org/archive/0636.htm

National Weather Service Forecast Office, Omaha/Valley, NE: Hallam Nebraska Tornado. http://www.crh.noaa.gov/oax/archive/hallam/hallam.php

National Weather Service Forecast Office, Springfield, MO: Joplin Tornado Survey. http://www.crh.noaa.gov/sgf/?n=event_2011may22_survey#Joplin

"Tornadoes: Nature's Most Violent Storms." National Severe Storms Laboratory (NSSL). http://www.nssl.noaa.gov/edu/safety/tornadoguide.html

Tornado Project Online. http://www.tornadoproject.com/

"Tornadoes." University of Illnois WW2010. http://ww2010.atmos.uiuc.edu/(Gh)/guides/mtr/svr/torn/home.rxml

"Tornado Season: Are You Ready?" University of Missouri Extension. http://extension.missouri.edu/p/EMW1019

The Science of Volcanoes

Introduction

Mysterious and frightening, unpredictable and capable of destroying entire cities in an instant, volcanoes have always fascinated and intrigued mankind. Ancient people came up with many stories and myths to explain them. Most civilizations thought Gods caused them. The Hawaiian people, for instance, have a myth about the goddess Pele. It says she lives in the volcano known as Kilauea and makes volcanoes erupt by striking the ground with a stick. A Greek myth claims that volcanoes were caused by Hephaistos, son of the Greek goddess Hera and the Greek god Zeus, who had a forge where he made weapons for the other gods (including Zeus's thunderbolts) located under Mount Olympus. Later, he became the Roman god "Volcanus," and the Romans believed his forge was located underneath the volcanoes Vesuvius and Aetna.

Today, however, we have a lot of information about volcanoes and scientists understand what they really are. We know, for instance, that volcanoes have been around for billions of years, almost as long as Earth has been in existence. We know their existence has helped to shape the earth by changing the land around them to form new mountains and islands. We know the reasons why volcanoes erupt and are learning more and more about volcanoes all of the time by studying them. Scientists currently study volcanoes in an effort to understand how to predict when they might erupt. This sort of knowledge will help to save lives in the future.

According to the Smithsonian Global Volcanism Program Institute, 50 – 70 volcanoes erupt each year around the world. There are approximately 20 volcanoes erupting somewhere right now as you read these words. They also count approximately 1,300 active volcanoes in the world today ("active" means that a volcano has erupted sometime in the past 10,000 years), and many more volcanoes that are "dormant" or "extinct" (which means they have not erupted for a very long time). These estimates do not include volcanoes on the ocean floor or volcanoes in outer space.

Most volcanoes are found along the edges of "tectonic plates" (massive slabs of lightweight rock that float on a layer of heavier rock) that make up the Earth's crust. When these plates shift and move apart, a volcano may erupt, spewing volcanic rock and gases to the Earth's surface.

Volcanoes are fascinating and cause a wide range of emotions in people, such as fear and admiration. They can erupt with great violence and carry the potential for complete devastation, since they are capable of wiping out entire cities in a day. But they also inspire awe due to their incredible size and age. They rise miles and miles above earth and are thousands and thousands of years old. What is behind these incredible landforms? How did they form and why do they erupt?

Chapter 1: What Is It?

A volcano is a mountain that is very different from other mountains because it has a hole, or "vent," through which hot material erupts from deep within the earth. The word "volcano" comes from the name of the island of Vulcano, which is located off the southwest coast of Italy. It is this island that the Romans believed was located above the forge of Vulcan, the god who made weapons for the other gods. The Romans believed the hot lava and dust erupting from vents on the island were the fumes and sparks created by Vulcan as he worked in his forge. The word "volcano" has since come to refer to the activity of molten rock, or magma, making its way through vents to the earth's surface, where it becomes lava.

The word "volcano" actually has two meanings, and what the word means depends on how it is used. It can be used to describe the landform – a mountain or crack – that has formed around a vent. The landform was built by the eruptions of lava from the vent. It can also be used to refer to the vent itself. The vent, which is like a chimney, leads all the way to the layer of magma (very hot, molten rock) deep within the Earth. Thick slabs of rock, called "tectonic plates," may block the vent. When tectonic plates shift, however, and move apart, the magma will bubble up and escape through the volcano's vent as a volcanic eruption.

The context in which the word "volcano" is used will help to determine which meaning is being implied. For instance, if someone says, "The volcano erupted with a violent blast of lava," the word "volcano" is being used to refer to the vent through which magma reaches the surface of the earth. However, if someone says, "Mount Olympus is the tallest volcano in the solar system," the word "volcano" is being used to refer to the landform built by eruptions.

Chapter 2: Types of Volcanoes

Volcanologists classify volcanoes into groups based on the materials that form them, the way they erupt, and their shape and size. The groups are shield volcanoes, stratovolcanoes, cinder cones, and complex volcanoes.

Shield Volcano

In a shield volcano, lava flows out of one or more vents (cracks) in the Earth's crust when the volcano erupts. The eruptions are quiet and the lava is free-flowing and very fluid. It is comprised almost exclusively of basalt (a type of volcanic rock) and can travel very fast. There is very little pyroclastic (fragmented) material in the lava. It is very hot and remains in the form in which it was originally generated. The lava spreads in all directions and hardens as it cools. Eventually, over hundreds of years, the hardened lava builds up into a broad, gently sloping cone. The cone looks like a warrior's shield, and that's where this type of volcano got its name. Many of the Hawaiian volcanoes, such as Mauna Loa and Kilauea, are good examples of shield volcanoes.

Shield Volcano

Stratovolcanoes

A stratovolcano is a tall, cone-shaped volcano that is created as eruptions of ash, lava, and cinders build up in layers. It has a wide base and a steep top. Stratovolcanoes are much steeper than shield volcanoes. The lava from stratovolcanoes is often "felsic," which means that is has fairly high levels of silica (a mineral contained in volcanic rock), and therefore has a high viscosity (thickness). Because of this, it is slow-moving and hardens before it spreads far. Stratovolcanoes have two kinds of eruptions – slow moving or violent. This causes them to be very unpredictable. They are sometimes referred to as "composite volcanoes," due to the many layers that form. Examples of stratovolcanoes are Areanl in Costa Rico and Stromboli in Italy. Vesuivius, which destroyed the cities of Pompeii and Herculaneum, was a stratovolcano.

Stratovolcano

Cinder Cones

Cinder cones, sometimes referred to as "scoria cones," form when a volcano vent spews lava cinders (melted volcanic rock that has cooled and formed into pebble-sized pieces) so that they spatter skyward. It has a very violent and explosive eruption and is considered to be the most dangerous type of volcano. The cinders, also known as "scoria," are comprised of rock fragments that are glassy and that contain many gas bubbles, due to the magma exploding into the air and then cooling quickly. After the cinders fall back to the surface of the earth, they form a steep, conical hill with a circular, bowl-shaped depression on top. Smaller and simpler than composite volcanoes, cinder cones are the most common form of volcano. They are often found on the flanks of shield volcanoes and stratovolcanoes. Examples of cinder cones are Cerro Negro in Nigeria and Paricutin in Mexico.

Cinder Cones

Complex Volcanoes

A complex volcano, sometimes referred to as a "compound volcano," consists of two or more volcanoes that have formed near one another. They may have multiple vents and summits that overlap. The separate features on complex volcanoes form at different times. Complex volcanoes often form when a hotspot (the area where magma rises to the earth's surface) shifts, causing a new cone and vent to form. Examples of complex volcanoes are Banahaw volcano in the Phillpines, which is a complex of three volcanoes – Banahaw, San Cristobal, and Banhao de Lucban – and Mount Kusatsu-Shirane in Japan, which is made up of a series of overlapping cones and three crater lakes.

Chapter 3: Classifying

There are three classifications for volcanoes: active, dormant, and extinct.

Active
When a volcano is classified as "active," it is said to be "live," and is either showing signs of unrest or is actively erupting. The Smithsonian Global Volcanism Program currently lists about 1,300 volcanoes considered as being active. These are volcanoes that are known to have erupted sometime in the last 10,000 years.

Dormant
When a volcano has not erupted for at least 600 years, it is considered "dormant." Although it is currently not erupting, it is considered to still be "live" and may erupt at any time. However, it may be on its way to becoming extinct, in which case it will not ever erupt again. Because volcanoes often remain inactive for thousands of years between eruptions, it can be difficult to distinguish whether a volcano is "dormant" or "extinct." Only time can determine when a volcano moves from the classification of "dormant" to the classification of "extinct."

Extinct
A volcano is "extinct" when it has stopped erupting altogether. Again, it is sometimes hard to tell whether a volcano is actually extinct or only dormant, as a volcano may be inactive for thousands of years and then suddenly erupt. A volcano is officially considered extinct only when it has been inactive for 10,000 years. An example of a volcano that is classified as extinct is Kohala in Hawaii, which has not erupted for over 60,000 years.

Volcanoes become extinct for several reasons. One reason is that the final eruption of the volcano is so explosive, it destroys the structure of the volcano. Another reason a volcano will become extinct is if the volcano moves when the tectonic plate on which it is located shifts and is thus cut off from its "hotspot" (its magma source). Meanwhile, the hotspot may create a new volcano.

U.S. Volcanic Activity Alert

The United States has approximately 170 active volcanoes within its borders. The Smithsonian's Global Volcanism Program and the U.S. Geological Survey's (USGS) Volcano Hazards Program have joined together to issue a "Weekly Volcanic Activity Report," which alerts people in the areas surrounding active volcanoes of any changes in recent activity. Through its five volcano observatories, the USGS issues information and warnings to the public about volcanic activity for approximately 50 U.S. volcanoes.
The notices are posted weekly.

The reports are based on information obtained from several sources, including seismic activity, satellite and web camera images, gas emission measurements, and eyewitness reports. Information on volcano activity is organized as "New Activity/Unrest" and "Ongoing Activity." The USGS also has a standardized alert-notification system and issues an "Aviation Color Code" to alert pilots flying in the area of a volcano. Green means that the volcano is in a non-active state. Yellow means the volcano is showing signs of elevated unrest. Orange means the volcano is showing signs of heightened unrest and eruption may be underway with no volcanic ash emissions. Red means that eruption is imminent with potential for significant emission of volcanic ash.

Measuring Volcanoes

There are several methods scientists use to measure volcanoes and these are always changing and evolving. One way is to visit the site of the volcano and study the volume of lava and ash the volcanic eruptions produce as well as the different types of gases that come out of volcanoes. This can be a time-consuming process and can take several months to accomplish.

Volcanologists use many types of tools to measure volcanic behavior, including seismometers (instruments that measure motions of the ground) to measure seismic waves around the volcano, Global Positioning System (GPS) to measure volcano ground deformation. Traditional surveying equipment, such as theodolites (surveying instruments that have a rotating telescope used to measure horizontal and vertical angles) and satellite imagery are used to measure the swelling and deflation of volcanoes.

Another way to measure how big a volcanic eruption is to use a Volcanic Explosively Index (VEI). It is a scale that provides a relative measure of the explosiveness of volcanic eruptions. The scale ranges from 0 (which is given for non-explosive eruptions) to 8 (which is given to the largest volcanoes in history). The VEI utilizes aspects such as "ejecta volume" (the amount of material that is ejected from the volcano), "plume" (the eruption cloud height), and frequency of eruption to determine the rating.

Chapter 4: How Do Volcanoes Work?

The earth is composed of several layers, including the crust, the upper mantle, the mantle, the outer core, and the inner core. These descend in order from the surface of the earth (the crust) to its center (the inner core). The earth's crust is made up of several "tectonic plates," or huge sections of earth that float on the mantle, a viscous (thick and sticky) layer that is located between the crust and the outer core. These tectonic plates are, on the average, 50 miles thick and are in constant motion relative to one another. A hot, mobile layer of partially molten rock (known as the "asthenosphere") lies within the earth's upper mantle beneath the tectonic plates (which are part of the "lithosphere," the rigid outer portion of the earth). When these plates shift, this layer of partially molten rock may rise to the earth's surface in the form of a volcanic eruption.

Sometimes the tectonic plates "diverge" (move away from one another), sometimes they "converge" (move toward one another), and sometimes they "transform" (slide past one another). The areas where these plates are moving toward one another, away from one another, or past one another are called "plate boundaries." Volcanoes are most abundant at divergent and convergent plate boundaries, with a distinct lack of significant volcano associated with transform plate boundaries. However, some active volcanoes are not associated with plate boundaries at all, such as the volcanic chain that comprises the Hawaiian Islands. These are known as "intra-plate" volcanoes and are generated by the presence of "hotspots," which are areas where there is a rising plume of magma that is not located at a plate boundary.

Divergent Plate Tectonics

Diverging plate boundaries are located mostly beneath the oceans as long volcanic rifts (a zone of volcanic cracks or openings) and are sometimes referred to as "oceanic ridges." These oceanic ridges erupt much more lava than volcanoes on land do – up to three times as much more.

Convergent Plate Tectonics

Convergent plates form collide to form new landforms, such as volcanoes and mountain ranges. The Cascade Range and the Himalaya were both created due to convergent plate tectonics. Individual volcanoes may form on the plate that triumphs when two plates collide. In other words, they may form on the plate that stays on top and does not "subduct," or go under the other.

Hotspots

A hotspot is an area where rising plumes of hot mantle reach the surface, usually at locations that are far away from plate boundaries. A volcano remains active as long as it is positioned above a hot spot, but when plates shift, the motion sometimes results in the volcano moving away from the plume of mantle and the volcano becomes extinct.

Volcano Features

Magma Chamber

A magma chamber is a large reservoir (or pool) of molten rock material beneath the surface of the Earth. They come in different shapes and are most often dome shaped or spherical. Magma chambers are located anywhere from 1 km to 10 km under the Earth's surface and range in dimension from hundreds of meters to hundreds of kilometers.

Scientists are able to determine the size and shape of a magma chamber by measuring seismic waves (waves of energy that travel through the earth and give off an acoustic energy). They can "build" a 3-D image of the magma chamber in the same way medical CT scans are used to build an image of body tissue inside a human by using X-rays. For instance, scientists know that the magma chamber currently located under Yellowstone is about 40 by 80 kilometers across; the top of it is 8 km below the surface of the earth and the bottom of it is about 16 km below the surface.

Magma rises into the magma chamber from beneath the earth's crust. As more and more magma rises, the pressure inside the chamber builds and, eventually, the magma blasts out of the magma chamber as a volcanic eruption.

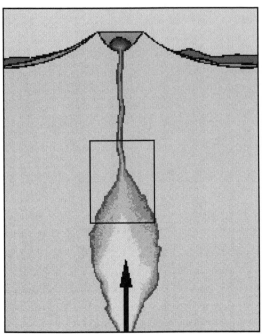

Magma Chamber

Main Vent

A magma chamber is connected to the earth's surface by a main vent, which is sometimes referred to as the "central vent." Most main vents are a single circular-shaped structure. Magma and volcanic gases travel through this vent to the surface, where they escape into the atmosphere as lava. The geological structure known as a volcano builds up around the vent as ash, rock and lava ejected during eruptions fall back to Earth. Most volcanoes have a circular central vent near the summit crater, and many also have secondary vents along their flanks, through which smaller eruptions of gases and lava occur. Secondary vents may be large long fissures (linear cracks). Some secondary vents are nothing more than a small crack in the ground.

If magma is sticky and thick, it may block a volcano's main vent. When this happens, volcanic gases build up behind the magma, causing the eventual eruption to be extremely explosive. These explosive eruptions tend to contain large clouds of rock particles instead of flowing lava. Occasionally, volcanic eruptions may be so violent they destroy the main vent. When this occurs, a new vent may form, as well as a new form of eruption due to the structural change.

Crater

The bowl-shaped or basin-like formation that forms at the mouth of the vent is known as the crater. It is created after a volcanic eruption collapses to form a depression. A crater is circular in shape and may be very wide and deep. Some craters may be "breached," which means they are lower on one side than the other. This can occur during volcanic eruption or it may be due to erosion.

A volcano crater is generally situated on top of a volcano at the summit, although sometimes craters may be positioned on the flanks of the volcano (these are known as "flank craters.") Craters sometimes fill with water or melted snow, and are then referred to as a "crater lake." A specific form of a crater lake is a "maar." These are broad, shallow water-filled depressions that form after a "phreatomagmatic" eruption, which occurs when ground water comes in contact with magma or lava during an eruption.

Sometimes the volcanic cone collapses and depresses down after a volcano's magma chamber has been emptied after a violent eruption, but this is not a crater. When this happens, it is known as a "caldera."

It is important to note that not all volcanoes form craters. Fissure volcanoes, for example, do not have craters.

Lava

Lava is the hot molten rock that bursts out of a volcano during an eruption. While it is still inside of the volcano, it is called "magma." But once it makes it to the surface of the earth, it is known as "lava." It is very hot when it first erupts from a volcano and can reach temperatures of up to 1, 200 degree C (2,192 degrees F).

There are several types of lava and they behave in different ways. The two most important properties of lava are its viscosity (how sticky or thick it is) and the amount of gases contained in it. Lava that has a very high viscosity will flow slower and trap a lot of gas bubbles inside. These types of lava tend to be associated with explosive eruptions. Lavas that have a low viscosity tend to flow easily and release gas bubbles so they are not trapped. Low viscosity lavas are associated with fast moving lava flows that hug the ground and travel downhill, spreading out as they go.

In addition to molten rock and dissolved gases, lava may also may contain other elements, including solid mineral crystals, fragments of exotic rocks, and pieces of lava that has previously solidified.

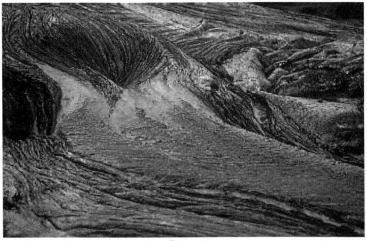

Lava

Pyroclastic flow

A pyroclastic flow is a hot, fast-moving mixture comprised of solid to semi-solid rock fragments and toxic, expanding gases that flows down the flank of a volcano. It can reach speeds up to 700 km per hour. Its speed is determined by several factors, including density and the gradient of the volcano flank. Larger pyroclastic flows can travel for hundreds of kilometers, although most travel under ten kilometers. They are very hot and may reach temperatures of over 1,000 degrees C. Considered the most deadly of all volcanic phenomena, they are usually the result of violent, explosive eruptions. A pyroclastic flow will destroy everything in its path.

Pyroclastic flows generally consist of two parts: the "basal flow," which hugs the ground and contains larger boulders and rock fragments, and an "ash cloud," which rises above it. Ash may fall from the cloud and spread downwind.

While pyroclastic flows are characteristic of many volcanoes, not all volcanoes have this feature. They are most common in plinian eruptions, which are marked by a high column of thick lava, ash, and gas that explodes high into the atmosphere, and vulcanian eruptions, which have a highly explosive nature due to the high level of silica in the magma.

Ash Cloud

Volcanic ash clouds are composed of pulverized rock, glass shards, and gases that have been blown very high into the air from a volcanic eruption. The rock particles and glass shards are very small – about the size of powder or sand – and are irregularly shaped with very jagged edges, which make the material sharp and abrasive.

The particles and shards form when magma that contains dissolved gas that is under extreme pressure bursts from a volcano vent during an eruption and the pressure on the gases is released. As the gases dissolve, they form bubbles that violently tear the magma apart, causing it to fragment into small pieces. These fragments solidify when they enter the atmosphere, becoming ash. This same process can occur if magma comes into contact with nearby water (such as streams or lakes). The interaction between the hot magma and cold water causes the water to rapidly expand and fragment the magma. Again, it turns into ash when it solidifies as it cools.

An ash cloud can rise high into the air in very little time. The ash cloud at the May 1980 eruption of Mt. Saint Helens, for instance, reached an altitude of 22 km in less than 10 minutes. Once the ash cloud is in the atmosphere, it can be carried great distances by wind. At the Mt. Saint Helens eruption, for example, winds carried the ash 440 km within 4 hours to the town of Spokane. The spreading ash cloud can have negative impact on many things, including human health, agriculture, buildings, transportation, and the environment.

Volcanic bombs

A volcanic bomb is a piece of rock that is ejected during a volcanic eruption that measures more than 64 mm in diameter (2.5 inches). Although it is viscous (partially molten) when it blasts out of the volcano, it cools and hardens before it hits the ground.
Many volcanic bombs take on rounded aerodynamic shapes while they are flying through the air and cooling. Some can be very large and travel a great distance. For instance, volcanic bombs ejected during the 1935 eruption of Mount Asama in Japan measured 5–6 m (16-20 feet) in diameter and were blasted a distance of up to 600 m (almost half a mile) from the volcano's vent. Not all volcanic eruptions contain volcanic rocks; they are most common in cinder cone eruptions.

There are several types of volcanic bombs. These include breadcrust bombs, ribbon bombs, spindle bombs, spheroidal bombs, and "cow-dung" bombs. If bombs are still partially molten when they hit the ground, they may partly fuse to form volcanic "spatter" (fragments of ejected molten lava that flatten and congeal on the ground). In some instances, if their outer surfaces are solidified and the interior is still partially molten, gas expansion and impact may cause the bombs to explode. However, this is rare. It most often occurs in breadcrust bombs that have a cracked skin.

Volcanic Bombs

Secondary Cone

A secondary cone, sometimes referred to as a "parasitic cone" or an "adventive cone," is the accumulation of volcanic material, such as lava and ash, which forms around a secondary vent. These sometimes develop on the flanks of a volcano. Each time the volcano erupts, more material bursts from the secondary vent and settles to form the secondary cone, exactly in the same way the original landform of the volcano formed.

If the solidified material plugs the vent, a new vent and thus a new secondary cone will then form. This process may repeat many times, forming a number of secondary cones. Larger volcanoes may have several secondary cones on their flanks. Mt. Etna in Sicily, for example, has over two hundred secondary cones. If the secondary vents do not become plugged, a secondary cone can become very large.

Given time, a secondary cone may eventually divert so much of the magma that it becomes the main vent and the original cone becomes less important. Mount Scott, for instance, in Crater Lake National Park in Oregon, is a secondary cone of Mount Mazama, a volcano that was destroyed by a volcanic eruption around 150 B.C. Mount Scott is 8,934 feet (2,723 m) tall.

Volcano Eruptions

When a volcano is active, it may erupt at any time. When it erupts, tons of molten rock, ash, rocks, or gases are forced up through it to the surface of the earth. The molten rock is very hot and burns everything in its path. An eruption is not always a huge explosion – sometimes the eruption is very quiet and the lava flows slowly.

A volcano eruption may be very brief or it may continue for years. A volcano ceases to erupt when there is no more molten rock left to come out of it.

Types of Eruptions

Hawaiian
Hawaiian eruptions occur when the magma erupts from a central point. They are named after Hawaii, which has many volcanoes that erupt in this manner.

Pelean

Pelean eruptions are named after Mount Peleé, located on the Caribbean island of Martinique. Pelean eruptions are characterized by the presence of lots of hot volcanic ash (fragments of pulverized rock, minerals, and volcanic glass) and a very fast speed. The explosion is often described as a "glowing cloud" as it moves down the side of the mountain and can reach speeds up to 450 mph. In a pelean eruption, the explosion of burning gas, dust, and ash looks like a glowing cloud as it races down the sides of the volcano.

Strombolian
Huge amounts of lava burst from a central crater in a Strombolian eruption. The ejected material consists of incandescent cinder, which creates sparks in the sky over the volcano, lapilli (stone-sized volcanic rocks) and volcanic bombs (a mass of molten rock larger than 2.5 inches). Strombolian eruptions are small to medium eruptions that are only mildly explosive.

Vulcanian
Named after Vulcano, the Roman god believed to forge weapons for other gods, Vulcanian eruptions are highly explosive. This is due to the high silica content of the magma. Silica is a chemical compound (formed when the element silicon combines with oxygen) that causes the magma to have a higher viscosity (the state of being thick and sticky). This makes the magma more resistant to flow. Because it is so thick, gases and pressure may build up behind it, resulting in a very explosive eruption. The eruption also forms a cloud near the volcano's top.

Plinian
Named after the Roman author "Pliny the Younger" who described the eruption of Mount Vesuvius in a letter, Plinian eruptions are characterized by a high column of thick lava, ash, and gas that explodes high into the air. The volcano ejects large amounts of pumice (a volcanic rock that is solidified frothy lava) and continuous gas blasts. This is the most dangerous type of eruption due to the phenomenon known as "pyroclastic flow," in which hot, dry rocks and burning gases pour down the volcano's side very fast. It is this type of eruption that destroyed the towns of Pompeii, Herculaneum, and Stabiae in 79 A.D. when Mount Vesuvius erupted.

What is Lava?

Lava is rock that is melted under the ground. Once it becomes magma (rock that has reached such a high temperature that it turns into liquid), and is pushed out of the volcano and on the surface of the earth, it is called lava.

All lava is very hot when it first erupts from a volcano, and can be anywhere from 700 degrees C (1,292 degrees F) up to 1,200 degree C (2,192 degrees F). It cools very quickly, at first, and forms a thin crust which then insulates its interior. The crust can become thick enough to walk on in very little time, but the lava beneath it may take several months to fully cool. It cools slower and slower as the crust thickens because it insulates the inside more and more as it thickens. Very thick lava flows may take years to cool entirely.

A "lava flow" is a mass of flowing or solidified lava. It can be so mild and quiet that is simply like a stream you can stand beside or so violently explosive that it can rip the volcano apart and cause destruction and devastation for several miles. The physical properties of the lava will determine which type it is.

Properties of Lava

The two most important properties of lava are its viscosity and the amount of gases dissolved in the liquid rock. "Viscosity," as we've noted, describes the stickiness and thickness of a lava. Some lavas can be very runny and thin, like honey or melted wax. These lavas are said to have "low viscosity." Low viscosity lava can travel very fast and spread great distances. Other lavas are very thick and pasty, and these lavas are said to be "high viscosity." They travel very slowly and can cool into rock before it even makes it down the flank of a volcano. They are so thick they can sometimes plug a volcano's vent. High viscosity lavas can trap pockets of gas within liquid rock and are often associated with very explosive and violent eruptions.

The viscosity of a lava depends on many factors, including how much silica the lava contains. The more silica the lava contains, the higher its viscosity it will. Lavas that contain 70% silica, for instance, are approximately 10 billion times thicker than lavas that contain only 50% silica. As you can see, just a small percentage of difference in the amount of silica a lava contains can make a huge difference!

In addition to viscosity, the amount of gas that is dissolved in the liquid rock also determines what type of lava it will become. Lavas contain several gases with the most important being water and carbon dioxide. These gases are dissolved inside the magma when it is deep within the earth, where pressure is extremely high (much higher than on the surface), and they become very soluble (liquefied). However, as the pressure reduces as the magma rises to the surface during an eruption, these dissolved gases "exolve" (separate from each other). When this happens, bubbles form in the magma. The amount of undissolved gases in the lava and the lava's viscosity will determine how the lava will behave during an eruption. For instance, if it has a low viscosity (is thin and runny) and has lots of undissolved gases (which will thus form lots of bubbles), the lava will be very frothy and will contain lava bombs and cinders. On the other hand, if it has a high viscosity (is very thick and sticky) and lots of undissolved gases, the bubbles formed as the gas exsolves cause the lava to become highly explosive instead of frothy, due to the thickness of the lava. In addition, the gas bubbles fragment the molten rock to form ash. This second example is the deadliest type of lava.

Texture

There are three basic types of lava flow:

'A'ā

In 'A'ā flows, the lava's surface is rough and jagged and has lots of clinkers (blocks of broken lava). Its interior is very dense. Walking across 'A'ā is difficult since it is strewn with so much loose debris. It is so sharp it can tear clothing and flesh.

'A'ā

Pāhoehoe
Pāhoehoe lava has a smooth, unbroken surface that is rounded and ropy. It is very easy to walk across because it is so smooth.

Pāhoehoe Flow

Pillow lava

Pillow lava is characteristic of underwater volcanic eruptions. It forms in a thick sequence of pillow-shaped masses that are, on the average, up to 1 m (3 feet) in diameter.

Chapter 5: What is Volcanic Rock?

Volcanic rocks are formed by the crystallization (the formation of crystals) of lava as it cools. The properties and the texture of various volcanic rocks are dependent on two factors: the type of magma the lava is composed of and the rate at which it cools.

Types of Magma

There are three types of magma and they vary in chemical composition dependent on which elements are the most abundant in the earth – particularly in regard to how much silicon dioxide (also known as silica) they contain – as well as gas content, temperature, and viscosity. The higher the viscosity and the gas content, the more explosive the lava is.

Basalt

Basalt magma contains 45-55% silica and is higher in iron and lower in potassium than the other types of magma. It has a low viscosity, a low gas content, and a temperature of 1000-1200 degrees C.

Andesite

Andesite magma contains 55-65% silica and has an intermediate iron and potassium content. It has an intermediate viscosity and gas content and a temperature of 800-1000 degrees C.

Rhyolite

Rhyolite magma contains 66-75% silica. It is low in iron and high in potassium. It has a high viscosity and gas content and a temperature of 650-800 degrees C.

Igneous Rocks

Igneous rocks can be classified into three chemical types: "felsic," "intermediate," and "mafic." The rocks are named based on their chemical composition and texture. Felsic rocks have a high silica content and are often associated with pyroclastic volcano eruptions. Felsic rocks tend to be fragmented and angular. Intermediate rocks are lower in silica, but have a higher magnesium and iron content. Intermediate rocks have a tendency to form "phenocrysts," or crystals. Mafic rocks are low in silica and high in iron and magnesium. They are commonly associated with shield volcanoes and often contain very well-formed phenocrysts.

Basalt

Basalt is a very common mafic volcanic rock with a low silica content. It is dark (usually black or gray), dense, and fine grained. Basalt cools quickly, and therefore contains only very small crystals.

Andesite

Andesite has an intermediate silica content, meaning it is higher in silica content than basalt, but lower in silica content than rhyolite. It is generally grey or red in color. Phenocrysts are often found in andesite.

Dacite

Dacite also has an intermediate silica content that falls between that of basalt and that of rhyolite. It is very fine-grained in texture and light gray to black in color. It tends to contain blocky phenocrysts.

Rhyolite

Rhyolite is a felsic volcanic rock with a high silica content. It is light gray in color and has a fine-grained to glassy texture. Rhyolites that cool quickly grow crystals, while those that cool slowly may have textures that are rounded, flowing, or riddled with small cavities.

Types of Volcanic Rock

While Basalts, Andesites, Dacites, and Rhyolites are all types of igneous rock, any may form one of the following types of volcanic rocks, depending on conditions present during eruption and cooling.

Obsidian

Rhyolites and dacites sometimes from obsidian, which can be brown or gray but is most commonly shiny black. It is hard and brittle with a very glassy texture and sharp edges. Obsidian is produced when felsic lava cools very quickly with very little crystal growth.

Pumice

Pumice rock is a vesicular rock, meaning it is filled with many "vesticules" (cavities). It is often formed during violent eruptions that contain lots of gas bubbles. The vesticules are created as the lava cools around the gas bubbles. Pumice is very light in weight and has a rough texture. The texture is a result of rapid cooling and depressurization, which freezes the bubbles in place. Pumice is usually formed from rhyolite, dacitic, or andesitic. It is commonly used during bathing to remove calloused (hardened) skin from feet and hands because of its rough texture.

Pyroclastic

Pyroclastic rocks are the product of explosive eruptions, which cause fragmentation (breaking apart) of magma. They are often felsic (high in silica) and are often the result of volcanic debris. Lapilli, volcanic bombs, and ash are all pyroclastic rocks.
Lapilli are pea-size to walnut-size pyroclasts, ranging from 2 – 64 mm (.079 – 2.5 inches) in diameter. They form as the lava travels through the air, and the result of often a spherical shape, such as teardrops, button-like rocks, or rocks shaped like dumbbells.

A volcanic bomb is larger than 64 mm (2.5 inches) in diameter. They come in many forms. "Breadcrust bombs" form when the outer surface of the bomb solidifies as it flies through the air. "Ribbon bombs" are cylindrical in shape, flat, and fluted along the their edges, which makes them look like ribbons. "Spindle bombs" have twisted ends caused by spinning in flight and are elongated and almond-shaped. "Spheroidal bombs" have a spherical shape. "Cow-dung" bombs are still fluid when they hit the ground and flatten out in an uneven shape, causing them to look like cow dung.

Chapter 6: What is Volcanic Ash?

Also a pyroclastic rock, volcanic ash consists of very fine-grained fragments less than 2 mm (.079 inches) in diameter. It contains a lot of broken glass shards, as well as small amounts of broken crystal and rock fragments.

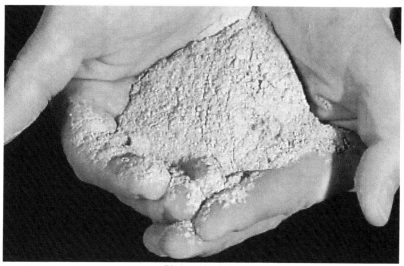

Volcanic Ash

Properties

Although volcanic ash appears to be soft, it is actually very abrasive due to the fragment of rock, glass, and crystal it contains. These fragments are very small but have sharp and jagged edges. Volcanic ash is vesicular in structure and contains many cavities. This gives it a low density that allows it to be carried high into the atmosphere during an eruption. Because it is so light and small, it can be carried long distances by the wind.

Volcanic ash does not dissolve in water. If it comes in contact with rain it will become gooey and thick. When it is wet, it will stick to roads and to the fur of animals. When it dries, it will be a solid, hard mass.

Dispersal

Volcanic ash is dispersed high into the air when a volcano erupts in the form of a column. Once it is in the air, wind will carry it easily, since it is so light. When wind spreads volcanic ash over an area, the ash is called an "ash cloud" or an "ash plume." It can be carried great distances. As it moves away from the volcano, ash is no longer kept aloft by the gases erupting from the volcano and begins to fall to the ground. The heaviest particles fall first, forming a layer of ash over the area surrounding the volcano.

Impacts

Volcanic ash can have several impacts on living beings after a volcanic eruption. It can cause respiratory problems for humans, including nose and throat irritation and coughing. The small, sharp ash particles can also cause eye irritation. These problems may also occur in animals. Additionally, it may cover an animal's food source, which will make the food inedible. Thick accumulations on crops and plants may damage them.

Volcanic ash also has an impact on inanimate objects. The weight of it can cause building roofs to collapse and it can clog gutters and drainpipes when it is wet. The fine ash particles can also cause damage to appliances and to the wires and towers of communication systems.

Volcanic ash also has a great impact on transportation. Not only does it limit visibility for drivers by covering the windshield and the road, accumulation on the road may result in a lack of traction, much in the same way as snow. It has the greatest impact on air transportation. It limits visibility for pilots in the air, covers markers on runways, and can even get sucked into a plane's engine and cause engine failure. Due to this, the International Civil Aviation Organization has a system in place to keep pilots and air traffic controllers informed of volcanic hazards.

Chapter 7: Other Types of Volcanoes

Underwater Volcanoes

Scientists estimate there are approximately 5, 000 active volcanoes on Earth that are located underwater. They account for about 75% of the planet's yearly output of lava. Many of these underwater volcanoes are located near divergent plate boundaries, which are also known as "ocean ridges." The type of lava extruded by these underwater volcanoes is basalt. It cools very quickly, due to the cold ocean water, and forms as pillow lava on the ocean floor.

These underwater volcanoes often form islands, such as the Hawaiian Islands. The volcanoes build up over time until they rise above the water level. The Big Island of Hawaii consists of five shield volcanoes (Hualalai, Kilauea, Kohala, Mauna Loa, and Mauna Kea). A new Hawaiian island, Lo'ihi, is currently forming under the ocean off the southeast coast. It will not reach the surface for several hundred thousand years.

Volcanoes on Other Planets

Astronomers have discovered the existence of volcanoes on other planets, including Venus and Mars. Venus has active volcanoes. The Magellan spacecraft, launched by NASA in 1989 to map the surface of Venus, discovered thousands of volcanoes on the planet. One of the volcanoes, known as Maat Mons, is active. The entire planet, in fact, is mostly covered with volcanic materials, such as vast lava plains (a wide area of lava flow found along the base of a compound volcano or on the flanks of shield volcanoes), fields of small lava domes (a mound of lava formed by the eruption of high-silica lava), and lava channels (areas created by low-viscosity lava that erupted at a high rate).

There are also several volcanoes on Mars. In fact, there are so many that the planet is divided into "volcanic provinces" so they can be easily referenced. The Tharsis region, located in the western hemisphere of the planet, contains some of the largest volcanoes in the solar system. Three enormous shield volcanoes – Ascraeus Mons, Pavonis Mons and Arsis Mons – are located in the northern part of the region. Alba Mons (formerly known as Alba Patera), the largest volcano on the planet in terms of area, is located in this region. The tallest volcano on any planet in the entire solar system, Olympus Mons, is also located in Tharsis. Olympus Mons is approximately 14 miles (22 kilometers) tall, which is almost three times taller than Earth's Mount Everest. To the west of the Tharsis region lays the volcanic region known as Elysium. It is much smaller than the Tharsis region and its volcanoes are believed to be different from the volcanoes in the Tharsis region. Their lava and rocks are of a different composition. The main volcanoes in the Elysium region are Elysium Mons, Hecates Tholus, and Albor Tholus. The volcanoes on Mars are very old – some are over three billion years old! All of the volcanoes on Mars are extinct.

Chapter 8: Ten Notable Volcanoes

- The world's largest active volcano is *Mauna Loa* in Hawaii. It is 13, 677 feet above sea level and its top is 56,000 feet above the base of the ocean floor. The volcano has erupted 33 times since 1843.

- One of the longest erupting volcanoes is *Stromboli* in Italy. It has been erupting every few minutes for over 2,000 years.

- *Mt. Vesuvius*, located above the Bay of Naples in southern Italy, has erupted at least 30 times. Its most famous eruption took place in A.D. 79, when a violent and long eruption covered the cities of Pompeii and Herculaneum.

- *Krakatoa*, located in Indonesia, erupted in 1883 with such explosiveness that the sound of it was reportedly heard thousands of miles away. It spewed flaming ash that incinerated homes and killed a great number of people instantly. Approximately 36,000 people died due to the eruption.

- *Mount Etna*, an active stratovolcano located on the east coast of Sicily, is the tallest active volcano in Europe at 3,329 m (10,922 feet) high. The volcano is one of the most active volcanoes in the world.

- *Mount St. Helens* in Oregon erupted for the first time in 120 years on May 18, 1980. It ejected hot ash 16 miles into the air, and the resulting ash plume eventually covered three states.

- The eruption of the Icelandic volcano *Eyjafjallajokull*, whose name means "Island Mountain Glacier," on April 14, 2010, resulted in one of the biggest ash clouds in recent times. The cloud hung over Europe for days, shutting down airports and stranding hundreds of thousands of passengers.

- In May 1902 *Mount Pelée*, located on the French Caribbean island of Martinique, erupted, killing close to 30,000 people as it wiped out the entire nearby city of St. Pierre. "Pelean" came to be used to describe the unique combination of ash and gas that created the violent eruption.

- *Tambora* is a huge volcano located on the island of Sumbawa in Indonesia. The volcano erupted in 1815 and produced an ash cloud so big, it lasted most of the summer of 1816 in North America and Europe. The eruption was also the deadliest in history, killing between 70,000 and 90,000 people.

- The largest volcano in the solar system is *Olympus Mons* on Mars. It's about the size of the state of Arizona and stands close to 90,000 feet high. The volcano has not erupted in millions of years.

Conclusion

Studying Volcanoes

Scientists that study volcanoes are called "volcanologists." They study volcanoes to try to learn how to predict when and why volcanoes erupt. Most of the work is done studying the remains of dead volcanoes or by monitoring volcanoes that are dormant but may become active again. Not only do volcanologists want to understand how and why volcanoes erupt and to predict eruptions, they also want to understand their impacts on humans and their environment.

Volcanologists utilize many tools while studying volcanoes, including special probes that can be used to collect samples of lava. Because they often work inside of volcanoes in temperatures as high as 1, 832 F (1,000 C), they wear protective suits and helmets. They also use cameras to take photographs of volcanoes and to film different kinds of eruptions in an attempt to learn more about volcanoes. To monitor the activity of a volcano, they utilize a range of special equipment, including Global Positioning System (GPS), traditional surveying equipment, sulfur dioxide correlation spectrometers (COSPEC), and satellite imagery. They use this equipment to monitor ground movements, measure volcanic gases, and to study volcanic rocks.

Volcano Safety

The best advice regarding volcano safety is to stay away from active volcanoes. Sometimes, however, this is not possible. If you live near an active volcano or are vacationing near one, keep an emergency kit that contains goggles, a mask, a flashlight, and a working, battery-operated radio. Know what the best evacuation route is for the area and keep gas in your car. If a volcano erupts, it is best to get in a car and evacuate the area.

If you have to remain in the area, be sure to have drinking water on hand in containers. Wear a gas mask and goggles to protect yourself from ash, and wear a long-sleeved shirt and pants to protect your arms and legs. Shut all of the windows and doors of the building you are in to keep ash out, and block the chimneys and any open vents. Make sure you have a first-aid kit on hand to treat burns.

Volcanoes carry great potential for devastating destruction. They can remain quiet for many years and then suddenly erupt. Understanding the mechanics of how they form and develop, knowing when they might erupt, and being advised of what steps to take when a volcano erupts all go a long way to help to save lives.

Made in the USA
San Bernardino, CA
30 November 2018